SECRETS FROM
THE BLACK VAULT

SECRETS FROM THE BLACK VAULT

THE ARMY'S PLAN FOR A MILITARY BASE ON THE MOON AND OTHER DECLASSIFIED DOCUMENTS THAT REWROTE HISTORY

John Greenewald, Jr.

ROWMAN & LITTLEFIELD
Lanham • Boulder • New York • London

Published by Rowman & Littlefield
A wholly owned subsidary of The Rowman & Littlefield Publishing Group, Inc.
4501 Forbes Boulevard, Suite 200, Lanham, Maryland 20706
www.rowman.com

6 Tinworth Street, London SE11 5AL, United Kingdom

Distributed by NATIONAL BOOK NETWORK

British Library Cataloguing in Publication Information Available

Library of Congress Cataloging-in-Publication Data

Names: Greenewald, John, Jr., author.
Title: Secrets from the black vault : the Army's plan for a military base
    on the Moon and other declassified documents that rewrote history / John
    Greenewald, Jr.
Other titles: Army's plan for a military base on the Moon and other
    declassified documents that rewrote history
Description: Lanham : Rowman & Littlefield, [2020] | Includes index. |
    Summary: "The history books are meant to give you verifiable history.
    The United States Government wants you to not question the narrative
    that, in some cases, has been written for more than a century. But
    sometimes, real facts emerge from declassified documents that challenge
    what you thought you knew."—Provided by publisher.
Identifiers: LCCN 2019048051 (print) | LCCN 2019048052 (ebook) | ISBN
    9781538134061 (paperback) | ISBN 9781538134078 (epub)
Subjects: LCSH: United States—History—Anecdotes. | Military
    research—United States—Anecdotes.
Classification: LCC E179 .G77 2020 (print) | LCC E179 (ebook) | DDC
    973—dc23
LC record available at https://lccn.loc.gov/2019048051
LC ebook record available at https://lccn.loc.gov/2019048052

∞™ The paper used in this publication meets the minimum requirements
of American National Standard for Information Sciences—Permanence of
Paper for Printed Library Materials, ANSI/NISO Z39.48-1992.

CONTENTS

CONTENTS

FIGURES

PREFACE

It's hard to believe that more than two decades have passed since I filed my first Freedom of Information Act (FOIA) request at the age of fifteen, but here I am. More than 2,000,000 pages later, and a heck of a lot of paper cuts, the requests keep flowing out to every government agency you can think of. This book is some of the best of the best on what has come back to me.

Plain and simple: I want answers and I always have. I began my journey as a teenager seeking answers to the government cover-up on UFOs, but the impatience I had as a youngster made me quickly bored waiting for those answers to come. So to bide my time, I began filing FOIA requests for other topics as well. Records pertaining to the assassination of President John F. Kennedy, historical records from World War II, secrets relating to our most classified pieces of technology, details about our nuclear arsenal, reports about the Central Intelligence Agency (CIA) and mind control, the illegal testing of biological agents on humans without their knowledge; it all became my interest. And it all became my target to uncover.

Yes, I should have been reading *Richard III* in high school English or trying to pass all my math tests, I get that. But my mind was elsewhere. I never like admitting I was not the best student in school, but that is my story. My focus on the government's deepest, darkest secrets makes me who I am today, and I am now okay with that.

This book is a culmination of some of the greatest documents that have come into my mailbox. Let me preface this entire exposé: I do not claim to have been the *first* and *sole* discoverer of each document that has ever been declassified, or that appears in this book. There have been amazing researchers that have utilized the FOIA throughout the years, and some of them began their quest for the truth before I was even born. So, my hat is tipped to all of those, either reading this book or writing their own, who have utilized this powerful tool to gain knowledge that quite possibly has never been gained before. However, my intention here is to bring the best of the best together for you to see in one book. In the end, I feel that you will see things are not always what they seem or what we are led to believe.

Despite some documents being released before, I am proud to say that many you are about to read had never been released prior to my requesting them. The feeling you get when you open an envelope, and a document is before you that has never seen the light of day before, is something I cannot describe. Documents contain history, emotion, and sometimes they display a malicious intent to misinform the general public. I understand they are just words that have been typed or handwritten on a photocopied piece of paper. But you need to look beyond that and underneath what I call a "surface story."

A "surface story" is a narrative that we are told to believe. Whether from our teachers, textbooks, scholars, politicians, or appointed government officials, we are told that certain things are not to be challenged. We should just know them to be true, and we should not ask questions that go against that.

This book is specifically written for those who want to challenge the "surface stories" we have all been taught. These records, in some cases, completely rewrite the history books. In other cases, they add chapters to the history books that we never knew were there. They detail events, people, projects, operations, and major milestones in our human history, often detailing a wildly different story than what we have all been led to believe.

After looking at millions of pages, I often forget that before July 4, 1966, every government and military record that was ever written was done so without the knowledge that one day, the public would have a right to request that document. Yes, it was July 4, America's birthday, when the 89th Congress passed the FOIA into law. Although not enacted until July 4, 1967, a year later, the world was forever changed at that moment.

President Lyndon Johnson had reservations about signing the law, as he felt that it would hinder various government agencies to do their jobs properly. However, he signed it into law in a nonpublic signing ceremony (am I the only one seeing the irony in it being nonpublic?) and it went into law the next year.

Since then, the law has gone through various changes in the form of amendments and important updates that keep up with the times. One example of what I mean by that is the "Electronic Freedom of Information Act" passed by President Bill Clinton in 1996. With the advancement of the internet, the "E-FOIA," as it is often referred to, required agencies to put online "electronic reading rooms" of documents and make certain documents available electronically that were created after the passing of the amendment; but it also extended the response time guidelines, offering the government more time to acknowledge requests. The amendment took the allowance of ten business days to respond and turned it into twenty business days.

In short, there have been many amendments to the FOIA, but the core of it has always remained the same. Citizens of the world (not just the United States) can request information from federal agencies. The information requested is then released to the public. However, there is a huge catch. There are nine exemption categories, and if that requested information falls within one—the documents are withheld either in part or in full. Therein lies the point where the game begins.

Although the FOIA, at its core, has a simplistic formula on how it should work, it's nowhere near simplistic when you add in these nine exemption categories along with the various games that are played on the side of the US government. Long wait times and runarounds are only a few of the tactics that may hinder the overall process. Despite that, there have been huge successes, and records have long been released to those who fight hard enough for them.

This book aims to highlight many of the records that have come out during this long tedious process. What you are about to read, in many cases, took me years to obtain. My intention with putting together a compilation book of documents is to take (collectively) decades' and decades' worth of waiting for records to come into my mailbox and put them all in a comprehensive form for easy (and quick) reference.

Let me put it this way: each time you turn a page in this book, it represents one year, three years, five years, a decade, or even fourteen and a half years that I had to wait for what the next page contains. That's right—fourteen and a half years I had to wait, which is my record as of the writing of this book, for a document to come to my mailbox after I requested it.

I wrote a fun article about that experience, based not on what the document contained but more so about what happened on the planet as I waited for the record to come. Nearly four presidential terms had passed; world events shaped human history; I had gone through nearly a decade and a half of my life's journey; and so on. Think about how much time that really is to wait.

Despite its shortcomings, the FOIA is an immensely powerful tool. It requires patience and tenacity, but I hope that these next chapters show not only that it works, but also that it rewrites the history books that we thought may have been set in stone. The FOIA has the power to change our perception on the US government, to alter our view of history, and to challenge our way of thinking. In some cases, it will change your mind entirely on what you thought you knew and what you thought you believed.

Ready for the journey? Let's begin . . .

I

AMERICA'S BIOLOGICAL ARSENAL

1

SECRET CONTRACTS
FOR THE
CEREAL MAKER

What is the first thing we all do when we get up in the morning? Most of us like to eat breakfast. If you are like me and my son Christian, you love to eat sugar-packed cereal. Whether it is Lucky Charms, Cinnamon Toast Crunch, or Count Chocula, cereal just brings out the kid in all of us. But what if I told you the maker of those cereals that we love to munch on was researching a weapon system for disseminating solid and liquid biological agents in the 1960s?

Hard to believe, but it's true. General Mills, the maker of some of our favorite breakfast foods, was involved with a secret program related to biological weapons. Let me first deal with some background, in case you are wondering just how a company like General Mills would even be considered for obtaining such a contract.

Back in the beginning days of the company, General Mills was founded when twenty-nine mills that had operated back in the mid- to late 1800s merged in June of 1928. This combined decades upon decades of milling skills, equipment, and infrastructure, which began to pave the way for what the company is known for today.

But through World War II, General Mills also had a "Mechanical Division" that was formed out of what was known as the Washburn Crosby Company. General Mills, which has an extensive history of their company published on their corporate website, notes that "Nine in ten employees worked on war-related projects so crucial that armed guards patrolled there."

This era of American history showed that it was not only General Mills that assisted with wartime efforts relating to manufacturing and production. Much of the American auto industry also shifted to help Uncle Sam with the creation and design of defense-related technology. According to a February 16, 1942, *LIFE* magazine article, production of automobiles came to a complete halt:

> At exactly 1:31 p.m. on Feb. 2, the last pleasure car that will be until the war is won rolled off the assembly line in Pontiac's Plant A. Other famous makers—Ford, Plymouth, Studebaker, and the rest—had already ended production. Now the $4,000,000,000-a-year auto industry had only one customer and only one boss—the US Government-at-war.

The automotive industry shifted to making war-related orders, which, although it sounds like a detrimental financial hit to their coffers, increased their revenue exponentially. Military contracts were incredibly lucrative. *Encyclopedia Britannica* details that from 1940 through 1945, American automotive firms made approximately twenty-nine billion dollars from the manufacturing of war-related items. This was the result of manufacturing 2,600,000 trucks, 660,000 jeeps, 60 percent of all tanks used in the war, all of the armored cars, and 85 percent of the military helmets and aerial bombs used. The war completely altered the history books when it came to not only automotive manufacturing but also other corporate giants that had found their own specialty niche.

That brings us back to General Mills. According to their own corporate history, General Mills' technicians even had designed a torpedo in the 1940s, which was known as the "jitterbug." It was designed to first miss an enemy target to seemingly give the impression of a miscalculation upon firing. However, the torpedo could then change its course, even making a U-turn, so it could return to its target for a successful hit.

It was highly advanced work, and an effort that spawned great relationships with the US military in the process. After the war, there was not much need for military equipment like jeeps and trucks, but the infrastructure that many corporations had built remained.

These specialized divisions would go on to continue to work with the US military and, in the case of General Mills, would begin working on various contracts. One such program was the manufacture of high-flying polyethylene, also known as plastic, balloons to send instruments into the stratosphere for scientific research.

The Office of Naval Research (ONR) made an agreement with General Mills under Contract Nonr 875(00). The endeavor, known as Project Sky-hook, was just one of a couple balloon research programs given to General Mills, which date back to the 1940s. Project Skyhook balloons could carry up to two hundred and fifty pounds of equipment to heights of more than 100,000 feet into the atmosphere.

Project Skyhook spawned many other programs that took the next steps in scientific discovery using this balloon technology. Project Churchy, which began in 1953, researched cosmic rays with balloons launched from the Galapagos Islands near the equator. This location on the Earth allowed for naval researchers to better collect data on high-energy cosmic ray par-ticles, as it would not have an excess of low-energy particles that exist at high altitudes.

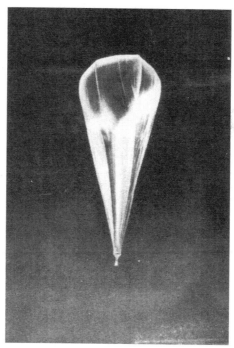

Figure 1.1. A General Mills twenty-foot bal-loon used in one of the test flights by the US military. *Credit*: US Air Force

Project Stratoscope, beginning in August of 1957, researched the Sun. Equipped with a twelve-inch telescope with a special light-sensitive system and camera, this program is believed to have been the first telescope to be placed on a balloon for scientific research. On the Naval History and Heritage Command's "Today in Naval History" website, Project Stratoscope is credited for obtaining sharp photographs of the Sun's corona from the first balloon-borne telescope camera.

However, scientific endeavors and discoveries were not the only aims for projects such as these. Behind the scenes in more classified settings, the technology was also being used and tested for something much more sensitive. According to General Mills as stated on their website, they began delivering balloons through their "Aeronautical Research Division," which had been established in 1946. These balloons were being delivered to the US military by the following year.

The US military learned early on that balloons would be a great way to collect intelligence about your enemy. One such program was known as Project Mogul, which began back in 1947. Although not a General Mills–led program, it utilized General Mills balloon technology. The effort showed the military shortly after World War II that balloons could be incredibly valuable for intelligence-collecting efforts. In the 1995 *Roswell Report: Fact versus Fiction in the New Mexico Desert*, Project Mogul is described as the following:

> Project MOGUL resulted from two important post–World War II priorities set by the Commanding General of the Army Air Forces, Henry H. "Hap" Arnold. These were to continue the cooperative wartime relationship between civilian research institutions and the military, and to maintain America's technological superiority, especially with respect to guarding against a bolt from the blue—in other words, a devastating surprise attack. MOGUL addressed both of these concerns. Developed partly under contract with leading scientific institutions—such as New York University (NYU), Woods Hole Oceanographic Institution, Columbia University, and the University of California at Los Angeles—MOGUL's objective was to develop a long-range system capable of detecting Soviet nuclear detonations and ballistic missile launches.

The report goes on to state:

Determining whether the Soviets were testing nuclear devices was of the highest national priority; it demanded the utmost secrecy if the information gained was to be useful. When the Soviets exploded their first atomic device in August 1949, the experimental Project MOGUL was not in operation. However, the explosion was detected by a specially equipped Air Force B-29 aircraft. Accordingly, MOGUL was conducted under stringent security-secluded laboratories, code words, maximum security clearances, and strictest enforcement of need-to-know rules. Nevertheless, while the nature of the project remained shrouded in secrecy, some of its operations obviously could not. The deployment of giant trains of balloons—over thirty research balloons and experimental sensors strung together and stretching more than 600 feet—could be neither disguised nor hidden from the public. Moreover, operational necessity required that these balloons be launched during daylight hours. It was therefore not surprising that these balloons were often mistaken for UFOs. In fact, MOGUL recovery crews often listened to broadcasts of UFO reports to assist them in their tracking operations.

Why the talk about UFOs? Project Mogul, according to the US military, was the culprit for the widespread story about a "flying saucer" that crashed in Roswell, New Mexico, in July of 1947. The military had changed their story multiple times about this popular UFO event, finally landing on the explanation that Project Mogul was to blame; not a "flying saucer." Of course, this remains highly contested, even by myself, which I outline more in my first book, *Inside the Black Vault: The Government's UFO Secrets Revealed*, but it is worth a mention. Project Mogul, Roswell-crash-related or not, was a highly classified program using balloon technology created by General Mills.

Project Genetrix was another prime example of military intelligence gathering using balloon technology. According to the National Geospatial-Intelligence Agency (NGA)'s document, published by the Office of the Historian, entitled, "NGA Reference Chronology," Project Genetrix is explained as the following:

OPERATION GENETRIX, authorized by President Eisenhower, used balloons with cameras to gather photographic intelligence over Soviet/Warsaw Pact and Chinese airspace. Although the operation produced valuable data, many of the balloons malfunctioned, were shot down, or released their photographic payloads in inaccessible areas. By the end of the operation in February 1956, only thirty-six of the 516 releases had been successfully recovered.

General Mills is mentioned more than sixty times in the *Roswell Report: Fact versus Fiction in the New Mexico Desert*, as it makes multiple references to their extensive balloon research and programs. It is evident, by this document alone, that General Mills, and the balloons they created, were an incredibly important aspect to military intelligence gathering.

Balloon technology, whether for scientific or military application, had major successes. But behind the scenes, it was a cereal maker that not only helped spearhead creating the technology that was used, but also that later would go on to make biological weapon delivery systems that would be carried by its own balloons.

In these programs, General Mills would focus on what they did best: milling and grinding. The cereals made by General Mills require intricate processes for grinding and milling special ingredients that make up their proprietary recipes. You do not just smash some grain or sledgehammer some sugar packets to mix it all together. Rather, it is a fine-tuned process to ensure that the result is a tasty morsel of sugar-packed goodness for the consumer at breakfast time.

When it comes to biological weapons—this perfected skill of milling and grinding cereal ingredients would become a valuable commodity for much more sinister programs. It was the process of making these cereals out of grain and wheat that made a company like General Mills the perfect contractor to take the lead in researching biological weapon delivery systems.

The contract was awarded by the Department of Defense and given to General Mills in early 1960. Little did the general public know at the time that the corporation responsible for boxing up their favorite cereals was now developing classified delivery systems for biological weapons.

This work came under contract DA-18-064-CML-2745. According to the first progress report, dated October 13, 1960, and prepared by General Mills, Inc., it states:

> This report covers the major areas of activity during the first three months of a program of research on dissemination of solid and liquid BW [biological weapon] agents. The objective toward which the research is directed is the development of weapon systems for the dissemination of these agents as a line source from high speed low-flying aircraft.

The problems of feeding and handling of finely divided solid agents were studied along with applications of feeding devices such as screw feeders, piston feeders, and pneumatic feeders.

Further into the first progress report, General Mills outlines exactly what the program aimed to achieve:

The ultimate objective toward which this research is directed is to provide weapon systems for dissemination of both solid and liquid BW agents as a line source from high speed low-flying manned and unmanned aircraft. These weapon systems will employ external disseminating stores, designed to be compatible with a variety of aircraft types, having speed capabilities above 0.70 Mach Number and low altitude.

At least fourteen progress reports exist that detail the work of General Mills and their biological weapon delivery system. The program began with milling and grinding harmless test material that they could load into canisters to see how fine-grained substances could be scattered around, let's say, over the enemy on a battlefield. Then, the program took the next steps for testing the actual delivery of such substances.

In progress report fourteen, published in 1964, the program had progressed through to loading test material onto an OV-1C "Mohawk" aircraft. General Mills had created a canister full of compacted talc and shipped it to Grumman Aircraft Engineering Corporation, which would handle the test with the OV-1C.

Despite these lucrative military contracts, the work of General Mills would eventually turn its focus back on the consumer. We know them in the twenty-first century as a food maker, and not a biological weapon research facility. According to their 2017 SEC 10-K corporate filing, General Mills has grown to employ approximately 38,000 people, with net sales topping fifteen and a half billion dollars. Their brands include Betty Crocker, Hamburger Helper, Cheerios, Pillsbury, and Wheaties, just to name a few. And to achieve all of that, it was their contributions to secret balloon programs spying on the Soviet Union and the development of a biological weapon delivery system that, at least in part, helped paved the way to what they are today.

Keep that all in mind the next time you walk down the grocery aisle. You will never look at breakfast the same way again.

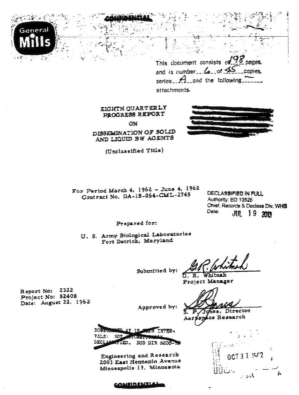

Figure 1.2. The cover page for the eighth quarterly progress report, submitted by General Mills, in contract DA-18-064-CML-2745. *Credit*: US Government

As corporations like General Mills were researching biological weapon delivery systems, and other classified concepts, there were other programs more sinister and more heavily classified. One hand of the military was seeking out delivery methods for their biological weapons; the other hand was testing chemical substances on their own.

2

TO TELL THE
TRUTH (SERUM)

When the US military began seeking ways to deliver biological weapons, it sought the help of some of the best in the business within the private sector. Companies like General Mills began receiving contracts to build weapon delivery systems to ensure the military had a proper way to fight a battle, especially if it were to turn into chemical warfare.

However, the overall scope of research was not only for using chemical and biological substances as a weapon. During this post–World War II era, rumors flew that the Soviet Union began experimenting with "truth drugs"—and they were making breakthroughs with the use of certain chemical substances as sort of a "truth serum." The fear was that any captured American soldier or intelligence officer would be injected with these biological concoctions, whatever they may be. The captured intelligence officer would be powerless to withhold the knowledge he had within his mind from getting into enemy hands. Any trained interrogator could extract battle plans, technological schematics, troop locations, weapon capabilities, classified information; whatever the human mind had within it was vulnerable.

This rumored capability was of grave concern to agencies like the Central Intelligence Agency (CIA), which was officially created in September of 1947. According to the National Security Council's Directive 10/2, approved on June 17, 1948, they called for covert action against the Soviet Union and granted authority to the CIA to carry out espionage activities abroad. As the months and years passed, the CIA immediately began infiltrating world societies; spying for America and sending back vital intelligence to ensure that the United States would remain secure and prepared for whatever the world would throw at it.

But what if these agents working abroad were the ones captured and subjected to the Soviet "truth serum" that had been rumored about? Their knowledge, background, and training would be susceptible to a skilled interrogator armed with a chemical injection; so, America had to act fast. Various branches of the US military and intelligence community began projects to see not only how to defend against such a tactic, if that was even possible, but also how America could use the techniques as well. If it works for our enemies, it will work for America.

PROJECT CHATTER

Project Chatter was one of the earliest projects that was carried out by the US Navy. Documents are scarce on the program, but it is referenced in the August 3, 1977, *Joint Hearing Before the Select Committee on Intelligence and the Subcommittee on Health and Scientific Research of the Committee on Human Resources* document, as released by the CIA. It states:

> Project CHATTER was a Navy program that began in the fall of 1947. Responding to reports of "amazing results" achieved by the Soviets in using "truth drugs," the program focused on the identification and testing of such drugs for use in interrogations and in the recruitment of agents. The research included laboratory experiments on animals and human subjects involving Anabasis aphylla, scopolamine and mescaline in order to determine their speech-inducing qualities. Overseas experiments were conducted as part of the project.
>
> The project expanded substantially during the Korean War, and ended shortly after the war, in 1953.

When attempting to seek documents on Project Chatter directly from the US Navy, they told me, by way of a Freedom of Information Act (FOIA) response letter, that the program was led "under the direction of Doctor Charles Savage of the Naval Medical Research Institute, Bethesda, Maryland, from 1947 to 1953." They referred me to a book by Martin A. Lee and Bruce Shlain, entitled, *Acid Dreams—The CIA, LSD and the Sixties Rebel-*

PROJECT MKULTRA, THE CIA'S PROGRAM OF
RESEARCH IN BEHAVIORAL MODIFICATION

JOINT HEARING
BEFORE THE
SELECT COMMITTEE ON INTELLIGENCE
AND THE
SUBCOMMITTEE ON
HEALTH AND SCIENTIFIC RESEARCH
OF THE
COMMITTEE ON HUMAN RESOURCES
UNITED STATES SENATE
NINETY-FIFTH CONGRESS
FIRST SESSION

AUGUST 3, 1977

Printed for the use of the Select Committee on Intelligence
and Committee on Human Resources

U.S. GOVERNMENT PRINTING OFFICE
96-408 O   WASHINGTON : 1977

For sale by the Superintendent of Documents, U.S. Government Printing Office
Washington, D.C. 20402
Stock No. 052-070-04357-1

Figure 2.1. The cover page for the *Joint Hearing Before the Select Committee on Intelligence and the Subcommittee on Health and Scientific Research of the Committee on Human Resources*, which outlined many of the human experimentations. *Credit*: US Government

lion. The book did not add much regarding the details on Project Chatter, which supports that there is not much available to paint an accurate picture of what it was all about.

It's important to note that whenever a US military or government agency gives you details in a FOIA response letter and references books and other nongovernment documents, it's never really a good sign. Usually, it is then followed by a response that indicates that they found very little, or even nothing at all, relating to that specific FOIA request.

In this case that I filed with the US Navy, wherein I requested all records on Project Chatter, it produced only one document. It was entitled, "Lysergic Acid Diethyl Amide (LSD-25) A Clinical-Psychological Study" by Navy Lt. Charles Savage. The FOIA letter already established that Lieutenant Savage (also a doctor) was the head of the program, but it was unclear at what stage of the program Lieutenant Savage created this report. It was dated September 9, 1951, which indicates it was about two years prior to the program's cancellation.

In the document, Lieutenant Savage details at least one portion of what some of these experiments were all about:

A study has been made of the effect of lysergic acid diethyl amide (LSD-25 Sandoz) or (LSD) on the affect, cognition and expression of "normal" control subjects and of depressed patients. It has already been shown by Stoll (1,2) that LSD has a pronounced psychic effect, manifested by increased emotional lability, dissociation, and imagery. Stoll described a euphoria which LSD occasionally produces in mental patients. It is the purpose of this present study to determine if such a euphoria might be of value in the treatment of depression.

Studies were done on 20 subjects, five "normal" controls and 15 depressed patients. (The sole criterion of "normalcy" was that the individual function adequately in his immediate life situation.) The "normal" controls were each given a single oral dose of 20 micrograms before breakfast. Psychological and physiological observations were carried out over a period of 8 to 15 hours.

The depressed patients were begun on an oral dose of 20 micrograms, which was increased daily up to a point where a definite psycho-physiological effect could be observed. This point varied in different patients from 20 to 100 micrograms. Psychological and physiological studies were carried out before, during and after the course of treatment with LSD. Treatment was carried out over a period of a month except where it had to be interrupted for medical reasons.

This last line becomes very important, as you will read in the coming pages and chapters.

What "medical reasons" could arise? Obviously, the US Navy was conducting tests on human subjects with LSD, and that in itself is a staggering revelation. But, what this document did not reveal is how much medical prescreening went into the program, to minimize the risk of medical complications.

Toward the end of the document, Lieutenant Savage summarizes his findings. He states:

Of 15 patients with depressive reactions, three recovered and four improved after one month's treatment with daily oral doses of 20–100mgm LSD. Four patients showed no improvement. In four cases, treatment was discontinued before proper evaluation could be made. Anxiety was a prominent reaction while less frequently euphoria was observed. In three patients who developed euphoria it serves as an aid to psychotherapy by encouraging expression of feeling. In the others the heightened anxiety encouraged reticence rather than confidence.

Improvement obtained during the course of LSD therapy was not greater than that obtained without its use in comparable cases. However, LSD affords therapeutically valuable insights into unconscious processes by the medium of the hallucinations it produces.

Despite the somewhat lackluster results, the program(s) would continue for another two years at the Naval Medical Research Institute, as it was established that Project Chatter was canceled in 1953. But it should be noted that the document does not refer to a "Project Chatter" although it was written by the established head of the program, from within the research institute the program resided in. Instead, the document refers to a "Project NM 001.056.06.02" on the cover page, however, it is undetermined if this was the identifying number for Project Chatter, or a different research program all together.

Why this is important is that although the US Navy provided the document in response to a FOIA request specifically asking for Project Chatter documents, it does not make it clear if it came from that specific program. This record offers the possibility that the navy was conducting multiple programs simultaneously, all researching psychedelic drugs like LSD and their effects on humans and animals. But, since this was the only responsive document, it may also indicate much has been destroyed or covered up about this era.

PROJECT BLUEBIRD

The US Navy was not the only agency experimenting with truth serums and drugs around this time frame. Shortly before Project Chatter was ending, the CIA had initiated Project Bluebird. According to an April 5, 1950, memorandum to the director of the CIA, the chief of the Inspection and Security Staff requested approval and authorization for the funding of a Project Bluebird. That authorization would be given, and it would start the CIA down a dark path of CIA programs that spanned decades.

According to this memorandum's attachment, it broke down what Project Bluebird entailed:

> The purpose of this project is to prove for the immediate establishment of interrogation teams for the operational support of OSO and OPC activities. The teams will utilize the polygraph, drugs, and hypnotism to attain the greatest results in interrogation techniques. It is important that this project be established inasmuch as a considerable public and government interest has recently developed in the use of hypnotism for interrogation and for personality control purposes. This interest stems from the recent spy trials in Hungary and other satellite countries. Within a number of areas of CIA there has developed considerable interest in the field of hypnotism and one of the basic purposes of this program is to bring all such interests within the purview and control of a single project. It is extremely important that any action by CIA in these fields be restricted to the knowledge of a minimum number of persons on a Top Secret basis to prevent compromise and unfavorable repercussions. Further, activities in this field are so highly specialized that untrained personnel should not experiment or attempt to apply the techniques of hypnotism under any circumstances. This project will provide highly qualified and technical personnel to perform all aspects of interrogation for all areas of the Agency.

PROJECT ARTICHOKE

Project Bluebird, as the scarce documentation reveals, was one of the first projects that dealt with a "truth serum"–like drug that could be administered during an interrogation, but it was by far not the last. About a year after Project Bluebird's inception, the CIA turned their sights onto a much more dark and sinister agenda. Those efforts became known as Project Artichoke.

Project Artichoke also experimented with special interrogation techniques using hypnosis and drugs including LSD. One declassified CIA report, previously "Secret," was entitled, "Potential New Agent for Unconventional Warfare," dated August 5, 1954. In it, the document breaks down the reason that LSD was important for research such as this.

> Lysergic acid diethylamide (LSD) (N, N-diethyllysergamide), a drug derived from ergot, is of great strategic significance as a potential agent in unconven-

POTENTIAL NEW AGENT FOR UNCONVENTIONAL WARFARE

Lysergic Acid Diethylamide (LSD)
(N, N-Diethyllysergamide)

Lysergic acid diethylamide (LSD) (N, N-diethyllysergamide), a drug derived from ergot, is of great strategic significance as a potential agent in unconventional warfare and in interrogations.* In effective doses, LSD is not lethal, nor does it have color, odor or taste. Since the effect of this drug is temporary in contrast to the fatal nerve agents, there are important strategic advantages for its use in certain operations. Possessing both a wide margin of safety and the requisite physiological properties, it is capable of rendering whole groups of people, including military forces, indifferent to their surroundings and situations, interfering with planning and judgment, and even creating apprehension, uncontrollable confusion and terror.

Of all substances now known to affect the mind, such as mescaline, harmine and others, LSD is by far the most potent. Very minute quantities (upwards of 30 millionths of a gram) create serious mental confusion and sensual disturbances, or render the mind temporarily susceptible to many types of influences. Administration of the drug produces in an individual such mental characteristics of schizophrenia as visual or auditory hallucinations and physiological reactions of dizziness, nausea, dilation of the pupils, and lachrymation. These reactions, however, are not necessarily obvious and only a trained observer, after giving psychological tests, may definitely ascertain that a psychogenic drug has been administered. Data, although still very limited, are available which indicate its usefulness for eliciting true, and accurate statements from subjects under its influence during interrogation. It also revives memories of past experiences. In at least one case there was complete amnesia of events during the effective period.

To date, no antidote nor specific counteragent is available. The effect of LSD may, however, be shortened in duration by the use of chlorpromazine, barbiturates, or the intravenous injection of glucose. Very limited methods of detection and identification are known, such as fluorescence, staining and spectrophotometry. Although the mechanism of action of this drug in the human body is not fully understood, it is nevertheless known to interfere with the carbohydrate metabolism and to affect the central nervous system, certain of the brain hormones, and other body functions.

*OBI is now completing a detailed study of LSD that will deal with the composition of the drug, its psychogenic properties, its development, experimental use, and distribution. This study entitled "Strategic Medical Significance of Lysergic Acid Diethylamide (LSD)" will be made available to those with a paramount interest in the subject.

-1-

Figure 2.2. A declassified report from the CIA outlining the important uses of LSD. *Credit*: Central Intelligence Agency (CIA)

tional warfare and in interrogations. In effective doses, LSD is not lethal, nor does it have color, odor, or taste. Since the effect of this drug is temporary in contrast to the fatal nerve agents, there are important strategic advantages for its use in certain operations. Possessing both a wide margin of safety and the requisite physiological properties, it is capable of rendering whole groups of people, including military forces, indifferent to their surroundings and situations, interfering with planning and judgment, and even creating apprehension, uncontrollable confusion and terror.

Of all substances now known to affect the mind, such as mescaline, harmine and others, LSD is by far the most potent. Very minute quantities (upwards of 30 millionths of a gram) create serious mental confusion and sensual disturbances, or render the mind temporarily susceptible to many types of influences. Administration of the drug produces in an individual such mental characteristics of schizophrenia as visual or auditory hallucinations and physiological reactions of dizziness, nausea, dilation of the pupils, and lachrymation. These reactions, however, are not necessarily obvious and only a trained observer, after giving psychological tests, may definitely ascertain that a psychogenic drug has been administered. Data, although still very limited, are available which indicate its usefulness for eliciting true and accurate statements from subjects under its influence during interrogation. It also revives memories of past experiences. In at least one case there was complete amnesia of events during the effective period.

To date, no antidote nor specific counteragent is available.

"Render the mind temporarily susceptible to many types of influences" was clearly the goal for the CIA. Allow the human mind to be infiltrated by interrogators or handlers, and make the subject do what they wanted. That would be the ultimate power to an intelligence agency such as the CIA. However, something new began to emerge along with various tests for susceptibility.

During Project Artichoke, they introduced a new aspect to this program that was not within the precursor program Project Bluebird: assassination. According to one document released to me by the CIA, it outlined a 1954 test that involved the Project Artichoke team. In a partially declassified, formerly "Top Secret" letter dated January 24, 1954, it outlines the first assignment of the program:

The Artichoke team visited [REDACTED] during period 8 January to 15 January 1954. The purpose of the visit was to give an evaluation of a hypothetical problem, namely: Can an individual of ****** descent be made to perform an act of attempted assassination involuntarily under the influence of ARTICHOKE?

Can that be right? The CIA was really looking into how to create an assassin who would, involuntarily, kill someone? It appeared so. And even more bizarre, why would an ethnicity (descent) matter to this "hypothetical" question that they aimed to answer?

It should also be noted that the one who wrote this typewritten letter used asterisks instead of filling in the blank of ethnic background. In their cover letter, they had stated that, "I have left blank certain identifying information which is known to [REDACTED]." It is unclear if they were referring to the asterisks they used, or if something else under the CIA redactions.

Regardless of that, just like in the 1962 film *The Manchurian Candidate*, starring Angela Lansbury and Frank Sinatra, the CIA was exploring the question of hypnotic and drug-induced assassins. The same document referenced went on to explore this "hypothetical" in much more detail:

As a "trigger mechanism" for a bigger project, it was proposed that an individual of ****** descent, approximately 35 years old, well educated, proficient in English and well established socially and politically in the ****** Government be induced under ARTICHOKE to perform an act, involuntarily, of attempted assassination against a prominent ****** politician or if necessary, against an American official. The SUBJECT was formerly in [REDACTED] employ but has since terminated and is now employed with the *** Government. According to all available information, the SUBJECT would offer no further cooperation with [REDACTED]. Access to the SUBJECT would be extremely limited, probably limited to a single social meeting. Because the SUBJECT is a heavy drinker, it was proposed that the individual could be surreptitiously drugged through the medium of an alcoholic cocktail at a social party, ARTICHOKE applied and the SUBJECT induced to perform the act of attempted assassination at some later date. All the above was to be accomplished at one involuntary uncontrolled social meeting. After the act of attempted assassination was performed, it was assumed that the SUBJECT would be taken into custody by the *** Government and thereby "disposed of." Other than personal reassurances by [REDACTED] ?eans (note: unreadable) of security involving the project, techniques, personnel and disposal of the SUBJECT were not indicated. Whether the proposed act of attempted assassination was carried out or not by the SUBJECT was of no great significance in relation to the overall project.

The most disturbing part of this "hypothetical" was the inclusion of an "American official" in the list of potential assassination targets. Regardless of this paper referencing a "hypothetical" scenario, why would it be necessary to include that?

The document ended with the conclusion:

a. In answer to the hypothetical question, can an individual of ****** descent be made to perform an act of attempted assassination, involuntarily, under ARTICHOKE, according to the above conditions, the answer in this case was probably "No" because of the limitations imposed operationally as follows:

1. The SUBJECT would be an involuntary and unwitting SUBJECT.
2. We would have none, or, at most, very limited physical control and custody of the SUBJECT.
3. Access to the SUBJECT is strictly limited to a social engagement among a mixed group of both cleared and uncleared personnel.

This was, according to the document, their "first assignment." Despite their conclusion that they may not be able to make that hypothetical person do their evil dirty work, the question arises how far did the second assignment go? The third assignment? Did all of these assignments stay "hypothetical"?

As you will discover in this book, document destruction has been one of the biggest hindrances to the investigative process, and when it comes to Projects Chatter, Bluebird, and Artichoke, that appears to directly apply. Prior to the passing of the FOIA, there was a lot less control over record keeping. Agency and department heads could, if they wanted, just throw the pages into burn bags to erase eras of history, and much of the CIA's dark past with truth serums and other drugs was lost to the shredders.

The documents referenced in this chapter are only some of the small number of remaining records that shed some light on this dark era of the intelligence community. As you will see in the next chapter, the three projects you just read about are just the tip of the iceberg. These programs are just a few on a long list of projects by the CIA that the CIA has tried to erase from their own history books.

3

THE CIA'S MIND CONTROL PROGRAM

The CIA was no doubt keeping a watchful eye on programs like Project Chatter, as that ended up spawning their agenda with Projects Bluebird and Artichoke. The fear that Soviet agents could potentially extract information from captured American operatives was palpable among the upper echelon of the intelligence community. But in addition to understanding how to defend against it, it would be obvious that anyone with an intelligence background would then want to understand the tactic and use it for an offensive move, as well. I'll say it again—if it works for our enemies, it will work for America.

MIND CONTROL

According to the 1994 Advisory Committee on Human Radiation Experiments report, sanctioned by President Bill Clinton, the committee gave insight on the CIA's involvement with mind control and what is referred to as MKULTRA.

> The CIA program, known principally by the code name MKULTRA, began in 1950 and was motivated largely in response to alleged Soviet, Chinese, and North Korean uses of mind-control techniques on US prisoners of war in Korea. Because most of the MKULTRA records were deliberately destroyed in 1973 by order of then-Director of Central Intelligence Richard Helms, it

Interim Report
of the
Advisory Committee
on
Human
Radiation
Experiments

October 21, 1994

DISCLAIMER

This report was prepared as an account of work sponsored by an agency of the United States Government. Neither the United States Government nor any agency thereof, nor any of their employees, makes any warranty, express or implied, or assumes any legal liability or responsibility for the accuracy, completeness, or usefulness of any information, apparatus, product, or process disclosed, or represents that its use would not infringe privately owned rights. Reference herein to any specific commercial product, process, or service by trade name, trademark, manufacturer, or otherwise does not necessarily constitute or imply its endorsement, recommendation, or favoring by the United States Government or any agency thereof. The views and opinions of authors expressed herein do not necessarily state or reflect those of the United States Government or any agency thereof.

MASTER

DISTRIBUTION OF THIS DOCUMENT IS UNLIMITED

Figure 3.1. In 1994, President Bill Clinton sanctioned the Advisory Committee on Human Radiation Experiments, which released their report the same year. This is a cover page from one of the original, interim reports by the committee. *Credit*: US Government

is impossible to have a complete understanding of the more than 150 individually funded research projects sponsored by MKULTRA and the related CIA programs. Central Intelligence Agency documents suggest that radiation was part of the MKULTRA program and that the agency considered and explored uses of radiation for these purposes. However, the documents that remain from MKULTRA, at least as currently brought to light, do not show that the CIA itself carried out any of these proposals on human subjects.

As evident with the above, documents have largely been destroyed to cover up the truth of what the CIA did with the MKULTRA experiments. Thankfully, however, it was not *all* lost to the paper shredders. Before we get there, it's important to understand how such a covert, sinister, and even in many ways illegal program would become public knowledge.

The Church Committee

Back in 1975, a US Senate select committee was established that was formally called the *United States Senate Select Committee to Study Governmental Operations with Respect to Intelligence Activities*. However, that mouthful was shortened, and it is better known as simply the "Church Committee," named after the chairman, Senator Frank Church of Idaho. The plan was straightforward; the group of senators would investigate alleged abuses of power by the CIA, the National Security Agency (NSA), the Federal Bureau of Investigation (FBI), and the Internal Revenue Service (IRS).

The result of the Church Committee's findings was published in April of 1976. It consisted of six books and detailed the abuses and allegations against the aforementioned government agencies. Although the complete details of findings do partially remain classified, one of the many things that was produced by the Church Committee was the existence of the CIA's mind control program known as MKULTRA. The details behind this program include the fact that the CIA was partaking in human experimentation, even on their own personnel, in hopes to further their research and their capability for intelligence gathering.

As mentioned earlier, the documents on MKULTRA were largely destroyed, by order of then-Director of the CIA Richard Helms in 1973 and the assistance of Dr. Sydney Gottlieb, the former head of the MKULTRA program. These papers were shredded just two years prior to the Church Committee convening, and the intent was clearly to shield the public from knowing the truth behind the program. What Helms could not destroy? Some of the people who were active on the program, and the Church Committee focused on their testimony to get as much of a picture about the program as they could. As a result of their persistence to find everyone involved, the Church Committee report outlined MKULTRA as the following:

Over the ten-year life of the program, many "additional avenues to the control of human behavior" were designated as appropriate for investigation under the MKULTRA charter. These include "radiation, electroshock, various fields of psychology, psychiatry, sociology, and anthropology, graphology, harassment substances, and paramilitary devices and materials."

The research and development of materials to be used for altering human behavior consisted of three phases: first, the search for materials suitable for study; second, laboratory testing on voluntary human subjects in various types of institutions; third, the application of MKULTRA materials in normal life settings.

The search for suitable materials was conducted through standing arrangements with specialists in universities, pharmaceutical houses, hospitals, state and federal institutions, and private research organizations. The annual grants of funds to these specialists were made under ostensible research foundation auspices, thereby concealing the CIA's interest from the specialist's institution.

It went on to state:

LSD was one of the materials tested in the MKULTRA program. The final phase of LSD testing involved surreptitious administration to unwitting non-volunteer subjects in normal life settings by undercover officers of the Bureau of Narcotics acting for the CIA.

The rationale for such testing was "that testing of materials under accepted scientific procedures fails to disclose the full pattern of reactions and attributions that may occur in operational situations."

If it is not clear at this point how some of the above can be construed as "mind control"—I will offer the following. Many equate mind control as the ability to make someone arise from their chair and bark like a dog. That was not the intent of the CIA's program.

With the combination of chemical substances like LSD and techniques like hypnosis, the CIA could extract information from the human mind. That was one of their many objective goals. In other words, you take control over the mind and bring down the natural walls and barriers that humans put up to stop saying everything that comes to mind. Intelligence officers went through vigorous training to achieve an even stronger ability to withhold the information they knew. The ability to withstand against torture was

The Director of Central Intelligence

Washington, D.C. 20505

The Honorable Daniel K. Inouye, Chairman
Select Committee on Intelligence
United States Senate
Washington, D.C. 20510

Dear Mr. Chairman:

During the course of 1975 when the Senate Committee, chaired by Senator Church, was investigating intelligence activities, the CIA was asked to produce documentation on a program of experimentation with the effect of drugs. Under this project conducted from 1953 to 1964 and known as "MK-ULTRA," tests were conducted on American citizens in some cases without their knowledge. The CIA, after searching for such documentation, reported that most of the documents on this matter have been destroyed. I find it my duty to report to you now that our continuing search for drug related, as well as other documents, has uncovered certain papers which bear on this matter. Let me hasten to add that I am persuaded that there was no previous attempt to conceal this material in the original 1975 exploration. The material recently discovered was in the retired archives filed under financial accounts and only uncovered by using extraordinary and extensive search efforts. In this connection, incidentally, I have personally commended the employee whose diligence produced this find.

Because the new material now on hand is primarily of a financial nature, it does not present a complete picture of the field of drug experimentation activity but it does provide more detail than was previously available to us. For example, the following types of activities were undertaken:

    a. Possible additional cases of drugs being tested on American citizens, without their knowledge.

    b. Research was undertaken on surreptitious methods of administering drugs.

    c. Some of the persons chosen for experimentation were drug addicts or alcoholics.

    d. Research into the development of a knockout or "K" drug was performed in conjunction with being done to develop pain killers for advanced cancer patients, and tests on such patients were carried out.

Figure 3.2. One of the many declassified memorandums regarding MKULTRA and numerous subprojects. Much of exactly what happened during these off-shoot programs and experiments has been destroyed and remains unknown. *Credit*: Central Intelligence Agency (CIA)

of prime importance to someone who knew too much and could become vulnerable in the field. The LSD, hypnosis, and other methods devised under MKULTRA intended to throw that training out the window.

New Files Are Found

The next year after the Church Committee published their findings, a FOIA request filed by John Marks, given case number F-76-374, yielded a discovery that no one expected, not even the CIA. The agency mysteriously discovered a cache of documents relating to MKULTRA that had survived the destructive actions by Dr. Gottlieb, by order of CIA director Helms, attempting to hide the truth.

In a 1977 memorandum to Stansfield Turner, the director of the CIA at that time, Mr. David S. Brandwein, Director of the Office of Technical Service, broke the news about the newly found records:

This memorandum is to advise you that additional MKULTRA documents have been discovered and to obtain your approval for follow-on actions required. Paragraph 7 contains a recommended course of action.

Paragraph 7 recommended the following:

There are now two actions that should be taken:

a. Release appropriately sanitized material to Mr. Marks' attorneys as required by FOIA litigation.
b. Inform the Senate Select Committee of the existence of the recently located records prior to informing Mr. Marks' attorneys.

It is recommended that you approve of both of these actions.

In addition to Mr. Brandwein's recommendations, the three-page memorandum also included some additional details, that would later be a black eye on the history of the CIA. In seemingly contradictory paragraphs, Mr. Brandwein stated:

3. (U/AIUO) At this writing, it does not appear that there is anything in these newly located files that would indicate the MKULTRA activities were more extensive or more controversial than indicated by the Senate Select (Church) Committee Report. If anything, the reverse is true; i.e., most of the nearly 200 subprojects are innocuous. This, the overview of MKULTRA is essentially unchanged. With two exceptions, the present find fills in some of the missing details.

4. (U/AIUO) One of these exceptions is Subproject Number 45 which concerns an activity that should have been reported earlier. That project deals with the search for a knockout drug which was a concomitant with, and a by-product of, cancer research at a major university. It is believed that an objective reading of that project would demonstrate the search for knockout materials and anesthetics were compatible activities. However, the research proposal stated that "chemical agents . . . will be subjected to clinical screening . . . on advanced cancer patients."

5. (C) Subproject Number 55 contains full details of CIA's contribution of $375,000 to the [REDACTED] Building Fund. The Agency was then involved in drug research programs, many of which were being conducted by [REDACTED] whose facilities were inadequate. In order to facilitate

the ongoing research programs, it was decided to expedite the building program by contributing to it through a mechanism that was also being used to fund some of the research projects.

The contribution could be controversial in that it was made through a mechanism making it appears to be a private donation. Private donations qualified for, and [REDACTED] received, an equal amount of Federal matching funds. A letter from the Office of General Counsel dated 21 February 1954 attesting to the legality of this funding is in the file.

What Mr. Brandwein was appearing to be minimizing in his memorandum is that there were "few" exceptions that changed the perceived overview of what MKULTRA was all about. Why this is incredibly important, even though only two exceptions were cited in the memorandum, is there are an untold number of documents, photographs, film reels, and like material about MKULTRA that were destroyed. Should those records have survived, it is unclear what atrocities would have been revealed and how they may have altered the perception of MKULTRA.

The astounding details of the program, through testimony, was jarring enough for the public to learn. But, these newly discovered records added even more damning evidence, and after multiple hearings, reports, and investigations, this was only the tip of the iceberg on what there was to learn about the CIA's involvement with mind control.

After Mr. Brandwein wrote his memorandum about the discovery, then CIA Director Turner wrote an undated letter to Senator Daniel Inouye, Chairman of the Select Committee on Intelligence. Director Turner broke the news:

During the course of 1975 when the Senate Committee, chaired by Senator Church, was investigating intelligence activities, the CIA was asked to produce documentation on a program of experimentation with the effect of drugs. Under this project conducted from 1953 to 1964 and known as "MK-ULTRA," tests were conducted on American citizens in some cases without their knowledge. The CIA, after searching for such documentation, reported that most of the documents on this matter have been destroyed. I find it my duty to report to you now that our continuing search for drug related, as well as other documents, has uncovered certain papers which bear on this matter. Let me hasten to add that I am persuaded that there was no previous attempt to conceal this material in the original 1975 exploration. The material recently discovered was in the retired archives filed under financial accounts and only uncovered by using extraordinary and extensive search efforts. In this connection, incidentally, I have personally commended the employee whose diligence produced this find.

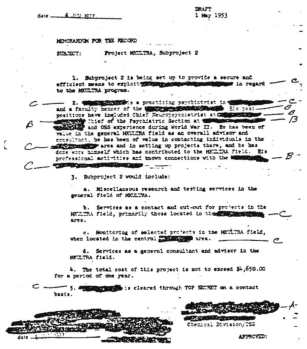

Figure 3.3. Undated letter from the Director of the Central Intelligence Agency (CIA) to Senator Daniel K. Inouye regarding the lost MKULTRA files that were recently discovered. *Credit*: Central Intelligence Agency (CIA)

Because the new material now on hand is primarily of a financial nature, it does not present a complete picture of the field of drug experimentation activity but it does provide more detail than was previously available to us. For example, the following types of activities were undertaken:

a. Possible additional cases of drugs being tested on American citizens, without their knowledge.

b. Research was undertaken on surreptitious methods of administering drugs.

c. Some of the persons chosen for experimentation were drug addicts or alcoholics.

d. Research into the development of a knockout or "K" drug was performed in conjunction with being done to develop pain killers for advanced cancer patients, and tests on such patients were carried out.

There is a possibility of an improper payment to a private institution.

The letter went on to state that the horrific subprojects of the MKULTRA program were ceased more than a decade prior and did not continue.

These newly discovered records in 1977, we would later find out, consisted of twenty thousand pages. They were ultimately released to the public, though sanitized and redacted. They gave a lot of details primarily about financials, but a small number detailed the subprojects and what MKULTRA dealt with and offered sporadic additional details.

In an interview taped by David Frost in Washington in May of 1978 and archived by the CIA to this day, former CIA Director Helms defended his order to destroy MKULTRA-related documents:

It was a conscious decision that there were a whole series of things that involved Americans who had helped us with the various aspects of this testing, with whom we had had a fiduciary relationship and whose participation we had agreed to keep secret. Since this was a time when both I and the fellow who had been in charge of the program were going to retire there was no reason to have the stuff around anymore. We kept faith with the people who had helped us and I see nothing wrong with that.

When asked about situations in which a director of the CIA would have a right to lie in the national interest, former Director Helms affirmed he could:

I don't think there is any question about that—just as other officials of the United States government would. I would suggest that if you unearth the transcript of the hearings of the Senate Foreign Relations Committee after the U-2 was shot down over Russia, you will find that there were very high members of the United States Government who were not telling the truth, the whole truth, and nothing but the truth. They were trying to protect the

President. He later admitted that he knew about the U-2 flight and revealed it. I am sure there are other examples of testimony before the Senate and House where the whole truth was not disgorged by members of the Executive Branch.

The Death of Dr. Frank Olson

If CIA directors, agency heads, politicians, and whomever feel it is okay to lie in the interest of "national security," then what can we do to ensure that our rights remain secure and we do not find ourselves the unwitting victims to some classified program within the massive intelligence community that operates today? One of the most painful aspects to MKULTRA was the testing on human subjects, in many cases, without their knowledge and consent. One such experiment was on November 27, 1953, in which the CIA gave doses of LSD in glasses of Cointreau to fellow CIA scientists and civilian employees working within the MKULTRA program. The test would ultimately lead to the death of Dr. Frank Olson nine days later.

Dr. Olson's participation in the MKULTRA program was due to his background as a biological warfare scientist and his work as a bacteriologist. He worked at the army's Camp Detrick, present-day Fort Detrick, located in Maryland. Without his knowledge, he was one of ten test subjects of the CIA experiment while attending a work-related conference by the CIA held in rural Deep Creek Lake, Maryland. The Church Committee report details the tragedy:

The most tragic result of the testing of LSD by the CIA was the death of Dr. Frank Olson, a civilian employee of the Army, who died on November 27, 1953. His death followed his participation in a CIA experiment with LSD. As part of this experiment, Olson unwittingly received approximately 70 micrograms of LSD in a glass of Cointreau he drank on November 19, 1953. The drug had been placed in the bottle by a CIA officer, Dr. Robert Lashbrook, as part of an experiment he and Dr. Sidney Gottlieb performed at a meeting of Army and CIA scientists.

Shortly after this experiment, Olson exhibited symptoms of paranoia and schizophrenia. Accompanied by Dr. Lashbrook, Olson sought psychiatric assistance in New York City from a physician, Dr. Harold Abramson, whose research on LSD had been funded indirectly by the CIA. While in New

York for treatment, Olson fell to his death from a tenth story window in the Statler Hotel.

It would be common sense that if a person exhibits paranoia, schizophrenia, and depression, he would need psychiatric help to ensure his road to recovery. Instead, the CIA did not take Dr. Olson to a psychiatrist, but rather, to someone close to them, who was cleared by the CIA to learn about the LSD aspect to the issue. His name was Dr. Harold Abramson, but he was not a psychiatrist. Instead, he was a pediatric allergist and immunologist.

During this time, MKULTRA and the LSD experiments were not common knowledge to the public. They were highly classified programs that could not have the details given to just any doctor. Rather, the CIA had to have strict control over who knew about the program and the details therein. In the case of MKULTRA and the botched experiment with Dr. Olson, the CIA settled to take him to a pediatric allergist and immunologist, simply because he was cleared by the CIA to be read in to the details of the program.

I will let you decide if the lack of proper care may have contributed to the death of Dr. Olson, but it certainly would not indicate he was getting the help he needed. In addition, there is one other aspect to Dr. Olson's death that you may not have realized yet, and the implication behind it is a controversy that has lasted for decades.

If you did not catch on to the details above, Dr. Lashbrook was the one who put the LSD into the bottle served to Dr. Olson and the other members of the conference (with the exception of two; one did not drink while the other had a heart condition). Dr. Lashbrook was also the one to accompany Dr. Olson to seek help in New York from Dr. Abramson. It was also Dr. Lashbrook that was "sleeping" in the same room as Dr. Olson when he allegedly plunged himself out the tenth-story window of the Statler Hotel.

According to details obtained by the Church Committee, on the night of his death, Dr. Olson was reported to have slipped out of a depression he was in that followed the experiment. Dr. Lashbrook himself testified that Dr. Olson, "appeared no longer particularly depressed, and almost the Dr. Olson I knew prior to the experiment." When they went to bed around 11:00 p.m. that evening, Dr. Lashbrook testified that Dr. Olson told him that he, "felt more relaxed and contented" than before they left to visit New York.

All seemed well, according to Dr. Lashbrook. That was, until the 2:30 a.m. crashing of a broken window that shook him awake. He then stated he saw that Dr. Olson had crashed through the window, falling to his death.

Dr. Olson's family was informed that he had committed suicide, but they did not know the details or specifics about what he was involved in. It would not be until 1975, when the US President's Commission on CIA Activities within the United States, or better known as the Rockefeller Commission, published their report. This commission was set up under President Gerald Ford and began just prior to the US Senate's investigation known as the Church Committee.

It was in this report that the Olson family discovered that their husband and father, Dr. Frank Olson, was subjected to the LSD test nine days prior to his death. After the family threatened to sue the agency over a "wrongful death," they accepted an offer by the US government that totaled $750,000 and formal apologies from President Ford and then-CIA Director William Colby.

Despite the settlement and formal apology, there has never been any final resolution to the idea the case was not a suicide. There are countless unanswered questions about it all, which plague not only the family, but all those who have concerns over what the US government and the military has done in the past.

As declassified documents have revealed, MKULTRA was only the tip of the iceberg of covert CIA-run operations testing drugs and other paraphernalia on unwilling victims. It seemed that quite possibly, these controversial tactics revealed in CIA files were just par for the course, as other declassified records prove that the US military began doing the exact same thing.

Instead of testing hallucinogenic drugs like the CIA, the US Navy began experimenting with biological and chemical agents. Their test subjects? American military personnel—some whom they had convinced to volunteer for the job and many who had no idea they were involved in the tests.

4

HUMAN GUINEA PIGS

The CIA made quite a habit of testing their newly found techniques on unwilling victims. The lengths they went to, literally around the globe, is largely a lost piece of history since many of the documents have been destroyed. However, they are not to be singled out for having played a role in such dark, sinister research programs that involved humans, whether directly or indirectly.

In a declassified report by the War Bureau of Consultants (WBC) Committee, which convened in 1941 by order of the US Secretary of War (present-day Secretary of Defense) Harry Stimson, the WBC stated the following about biological warfare:

> The value of biological warfare will be a debatable question until it has been clearly proven or disproven by experience. The wide assumption is that any method which appears to offer advantages to a nation at war will be vigorously employed by that nation. There is but one logical course to pursue, namely, to study the possibilities of such warfare from every angle, make every preparation for reducing its effectiveness, and thereby reduce the likelihood of its use.

To study "every angle" and grasp the ramifications of future biological attacks, humans were often the subjects of experiments by the US government and military. Sometimes the human guinea pigs were intentionally inserted into these nefarious programs; while other times, they were simply "caught up in the crossfire" and were made guinea pigs just by pure (un)luck. Military servicemen and servicewomen were not immune, and the experiments often involved unknowing civilians as well.

OPERATION DEW

Operation Dew took place from 1951 through 1952. It involved two different trials in the field, known as Dew I and Dew II. The aim of the program was to study the behavior of aerosol-released biological or chemical agents.

Very little is known about these early programs, as many of the reports, if they still exist, are still classified or considered lost. In a 1997 study by the National Academy of Sciences (NAS) entitled, "Toxicologic Assessment of the Army's Zinc Cadmium Sulfide Dispersion Tests," both of the Dew trials are described with little detail:

> The operation off Georgia, North Carolina, and South Carolina is referred to as Operation DEW I. The reference given is the document in Ref. 8 (Dugway Special Report 162).
>
> An operation named Operation DEW II, involving release of FP and Lycopodium spores from an aircraft. This is Dugway Special Report 179 ("An Experimental Study of Long Range Aerosol Cloud Travel Involving Ground Deposition of Biological Spore Material," F&MR Division, Camp Detrick, Frederick, Md., 1 June 1953) and appears to be the second (classified) document in Ref. 8 (not available).

During the Dew I trial alone, 250 pounds of fluorescent tracer particles, or zinc cadmium sulfide, was released into the air, affecting more than sixty-thousand square miles of the southeast United States, primarily in Georgia, North Carolina, and South Carolina.

Also in the above referenced report, the reason to use zinc cadmium sulfide was described in detail:

> Zinc cadmium sulfide is not itself a biologic weapon, but it was used as a tracer to simulate the dispersion of biologic weapons in various environments. It is an inorganic compound composed of the elements zinc, cadmium, and sulfur. It glows bright yellow or green when placed under ultraviolet light, so it

could easily be detected. At the time of the tests, zinc cadmium sulfide was thought to be nontoxic to humans, animals, and plants.

The zinc cadmium sulfide tests remained classified until the end of the Cold War. When the tests became public knowledge in the early 1990s, people in cities and towns where the tests had occurred began to ask whether a variety of health problems that they or others had experienced—including cancer and infertility—were related to exposures to zinc cadmium sulfide.

This report by the NAS serves as one of the few resources to understand the programs outlined in this chapter. The study was requested by Congress, as there were growing concerns that even though the zinc cadmium sulfide was considered harmless at the time it was used, there were ideas that it was not completely innocuous as previously thought. The report explains:

Congress asked the National Research Council to determine independently whether exposures to zinc cadmium sulfide from the Army's tests had caused any adverse health effects. The National Research Council, a non-government and nonpartisan organization that examines issues of science and technology, formed a subcommittee of the Committee on Toxicology in the Board on Environmental Studies and Toxicology to conduct the study. The subcommittee consisted of 15 people from universities, laboratories, private consultants, consumer groups, risk communicators, public-health agencies, and nongovernment organizations. Members of the subcommittee were chosen for distinguished expertise in toxicology, medicine, epidemiology, chemistry, environmental health, risk assessment, and risk communication. They served without compensation as a public service.

Operation Dew paved the way for more research in the years to come. Future programs would take the results from studies like Dew I and Dew II and build off them to further understand biological warfare. Not only for defensive purposes, but offensive as well.

OPERATION LAC

Operation LAC was a program that began shortly after Operation Dew in the 1950s by the US Army Chemical Corps. The aim was to simulate a biological attack to see how far an agent could disperse in the atmosphere and affect a large populated area. In other words, if a chemical weapon was used over a large city like Los Angeles, how far would the agent travel and potentially infect people with whatever agent was used.

Also in the above mentioned 1997 NAS report, Operation LAC was described as the following:

LAC, which took its name from "Large Area Coverage," was the largest test ever undertaken by the Chemical Corps. The test area covered the United States from the Rockies to the Atlantic, and from Canada to the Gulf of Mexico. The tests proved the feasibility of covering large areas (thousands of square miles) of a country with BW agents. Many scientists and officers had believed this possible, but LAC provided the first proof.

Figure 4.1.   Operation LAC utilized the C-119 "Flying Boxcar" to disperse zinc cadmium sulfide in massive quantities. *Credit*: **Department of Defense (DOD)**

Like Operation Dew, Operation LAC also used zinc cadmium sulfide during the experiments. It was dispersed by the *ton* from a C-119 "Flying Boxcar" on loan from the US Air Force. Many details about Operation LAC are not found in declassified American files, but rather, Canadian archives. The reason being is that when the C-119 would drop such massive amounts of the zinc cadmium sulfide, atmospheric conditions such as wind would take it over Canadian airspace, thus, affecting residents there.

In addition to the zinc cadmium sulfide, Operation LAC also introduced the *Bacillus globigii* to the potent cocktail of test elements. At the time of these specific programs, *Bacillus globigii* was used because the US military felt that there was "little health consequence" to humans. However, since this time, *Bacillus globigii* is now considered a "pathogen," or more specifically, a spore that can cause disease to humans. In other words, the assumptions on it being relatively safe to the sailors they were testing on were wrong.

PROJECT 112/PROJECT SHAD

The US Navy also took part in experiments that put lives in danger. One such program was Project 112. Project 112 was a chemical and biological weapon experimentation program, which was conducted by the Department of Defense from 1962 through 1973. This program involved tests on land, and at sea, which the latter went by the code name Project SHAD. Both projects, very much viewed as the same with only a different field where the tests were conducted, remained highly classified up until May of 2000. At this time, CBS Evening News ran stories produced by investigative journalist Eric Longabardi, who for six years attempted to find out if there was truth behind the rumors of the Project 112 and Project SHAD experiments.

Once CBS Evening News ran these stories, this forced the Department of Veterans Affairs (VA), along with the Department of Defense (DOD), to launch investigations into the claims. This then led to a hearing before the Subcommittee on Health of the Committee on Veterans' Affairs, held October 9, 2002.

In the official congressional record for this hearing, a statement was offered by William Winkenwerder Jr., Assistant Secretary of Defense for Health Affairs. He offered an in-depth history into the program, and his statement read, in part:

> An agenda for Project 112 was soon established to be overseen by scientists at the Deseret Test Center. A subset of Project 112 was a series of tests done at sea known as Project SHAD or shipboard hazard and defense. The purpose

of the SHAD test was to identify US war ships vulnerabilities to attacks with biological or chemical warfare agents and to develop procedures to respond to such attacks while maintaining a warfighting capability.

The purpose of the land based tests was to learn more about how chemical and biological agents behaved under a variety of climatic, environmental and different use conditions. Here's what we know today about these operational tests. The Department planned 134 tests under Project 112. Of these 134 tests, we know today that 62 of these tests were in fact canceled and never performed. We know that 46 tests did take place, that leaves 26 remaining planned tests, although preliminary findings suggest that most of these tests were in fact probably not performed. We will have more information on that, we hope, in the very near future.

Of the 46 tests that were completed, we now have released information on 37 of them and have turned the medical information over to the VA. For five we continue to seek the final reports, an additional four are pending review. We are attempting here to release as much information quickly as we can purely as it comes out and is made available. We did not want to wait until the end until all of it was available to us.

Documents on these programs and experiments are scarce, but some have come out to shed some light on the research. For example, declassified documents reveal that a test was conducted nicknamed AUTUMN GOLD on May 3, 1963. According to the heavily redacted final report of the test:

Deseret Test Center test 63-2, AUTUMN GOLD (U), was conducted in the vicinity of the Hawaiian Islands during the period 3 May 1963 to 31 May 1963. The purpose of the test was to determine the degree of penetration of representative fleet ships, operating under three different material readiness conditions, by a simulant biological aerosol released from an operational weapon system.

The report then gave specific details of the test, though much of the information is redacted. The following excerpt is cobbled together from multiple sections of the report, and I refrained from showing the lengthy redacted portions:

Test Program DTCTP 63-2, AUTUMN GOLD (U), was conducted in three phases, consisting of three trials each, or nine trials total. In each trial, two

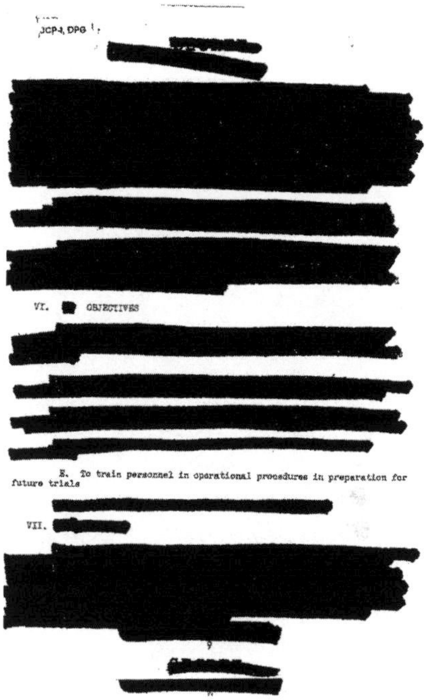

Figure 4.2. Information involving many of the tests, like this document detailing the Autumn Gold exercise, remain highly classified. *Credit*: Department of Defense (DOD)

A4B jet aircraft, each equipped with two modified Aero 14B spray tanks. [They] disseminated tracer BG (*Bacillus globigii*) along a release line. The Navy Mark IV and Army M17 protective masks were tested to determine mask leakage.

The four target ships listed below were assigned by the US Navy as typical operational fleet ships.

These ships included the USS *Navarro*, USS *Tioga County*, USS *Carpenter*, and the USS *Hoel*. The report then offered some details of the ships' personnel, and how some were informed of the testing being performed:

Personnel on each ship were briefed on procedures for pretrial exercises and the need was stressed for attaining the three material readiness conditions during the pretrial training exercises and subsequent trials. Ship personnel conducted these exercises and inspections prior to the AUTUMN GOLD (U) trials to determine each ship's capability to fully attain these readiness conditions under its present condition. [REDACTED] [REDACTED] [REDACTED] [REDACTED] [REDACTED] Navy personnel from each ship were assigned to operate the various sampling equipment on the ship. These men were trained during the week prior to the first trial.

Another series of tests, performed August through September of 1965, was nicknamed FEARLESS JOHNNY. In the heavily redacted final report, dated November 1966, FEARLESS JOHNNY had the following objectives:

> The test was designed to (1) evaluated for three material readiness conditions the magnitude of interior and exterior contamination from an aerial-delivered aerosol chemical weapon system using a simulant for agent VX, (2) demonstrate the effectiveness of the shipboard water washdown system for decontamination and as a protective measure against an aerial spray of agent VX, and (3) evaluate the operational impact of gross VX contamination on a US Navy ship.

The VX chemical warfare agent is an odorless and tasteless oily liquid developed in the United Kingdom in the early 1950s. The Center for Disease Control (CDC) describes VX as "a human-made chemical warfare agent classified as a nerve agent. Nerve agents are the most toxic and rapidly acting of the known chemical warfare agents. They are similar to pesticides (insect killing chemicals) called organophosphates in terms of how they work and what kinds of harmful effects they cause."

VX is considered by the CDC to be the "most potent" of all nerve agents, so what could they use to simulate it during the FEARLESS JOHNNY tests? They used a dyed Diethyl phthalate in order to simulate the VX, but even though they were "simulating" a toxic nerve agent, their simulant was not entirely safe and sound for the environment or for humans as it was used during the FEARLESS JOHNNY tests.

According to the National Institutes of Health (NIH), National Center for Biotechnology Information, Diethyl phthalate, "is a clear, colorless liquid without significant odor. Denser than water and insoluble in water. Hence sinks in water. Primary hazard is to the environment. Spread to the environment should be immediately stopped. Easily penetrates soil, contaminates groundwater and nearby waterways. Flash point 325°F. Severely irritates eyes and mildly irritates skin."

It was later determined that the military did not only use VX *simulants* during the testing phases, but also the dangerous nerve agent itself. In fact,

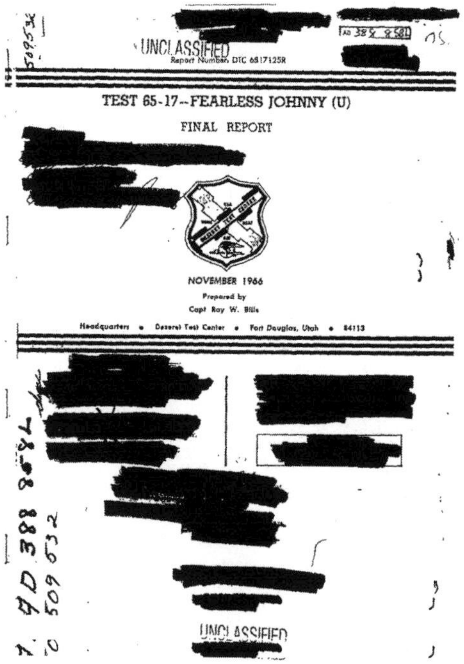

Figure 4.3. The cover page for the Fearless Johnny test during Project SHAD. *Credit*: Department of Defense (DOD)

there were eighteen total toxicological and biological agents utilized, that came in contact in some way, with the 5,800 military personnel that took part over the course of approximately eleven years. The complete list includes the following:

1. *Bacillus globigii* (*BG*)
2. Betapropiolactone (beta-propiolactone; BPL)
3. Bis Hydrogen Phosphite (BHP)
4. Calcofluor
5. *Coxiella burnetii* (*CB*; Q fever)
6. Diethyl phthalate (DEP or D)
7. *Escherichia coli* [*E. coli*]
8. Methyl Acetoacetate (MAA)
9. Phosphorus-32 [32P]
10. Sarin
11. *Serratia marcescens* (*SM*)
12. Staphylococcal Enterotoxin Type B (SEB)

13. Sulfur Dioxide (SO2)
14. Trioctyl Phosphate (TEHP or TOF)
15. *Pasteurella tularensis* (*Francisella tularensis*)
16. Uranine
17. VX Nerve Agent (VX)
18. Zinc Cadmium Sulfide (ZnCdS)

Each one of the eighteen on this list deserves a lengthy explanation to detail the breakdown, composition, effects, and dangers that some of them pose. I chose only a couple to highlight, in order to display how dangerous these tests really were, and how the various phases of the program played out.

The outrage by the public that prompted the 2002 congressional hearing was partially sparked by the inclusion of a few of these compounds and biological agents on this list. A year after the public was made aware of Projects 112 and SHAD, CBS News and the Associated Press continued their reporting, and on July 1, 2003, published an article that outlined continued secrecy and cover-up of this issue. They stated:

> The Pentagon is continuing to withhold documents on Cold War chemical and biological weapons tests that used unsuspecting sailors as "human samplers" after telling Congress it had released all medically relevant information.
>
> The Vietnam Veterans of America is suing Pentagon officials on behalf of the sailors, demanding the release of all of the test documents so the National Academ[y] of Science can fully analyze the potential health effects.
>
> Douglas Rosinski, an attorney working with the veterans group on behalf of the soldiers, said the effects of the chemicals on the sailors has not been studied. The levels of exposure that the documents might detail is a crucial piece of the puzzle, he said.

There was, at the time this CBS News article was published, an ongoing study initiated by the US government. However, the results were not finished, as it was part of a three-year, three-million-dollar contract with the Institute of Medicine, Medical Follow-up Agency of the National Academy of Sciences awarded on September 30, 2002. The aim was to evaluate the long-term health issues, if any, from the Project SHAD experiments. The results of this study were published in 2007 and totaled nearly one hundred and fifty pages. After their extensive review, their conclusion stated the following, in part:

> In conclusion, we saw no difference in all-cause mortality between Project SHAD participants and nonparticipant controls, and although participants had a statistically significantly higher risk of death due to heart disease, that lack of cardiovascular risk factor data as well as biological plausibility makes this latter difference difficult to interpret. We found overall deaths rates that were higher in both all participants and all controls than the US population, as well as a higher cancer death rate among all controls, mostly attributable to lung cancer. We also found overall worse reported health in participants, but no consistent, specific, clinically significant patterns of ill health.

What sticks out to me, is that you read there was "no difference" between the mortality of the Project SHAD participants and "controls" or those they compared them to that did not participate in the SHAD experiments. Yet, in the same sentence, it says there was a statistically "higher risk of death" due to "heart disease." Does that not mean, by definition, that there was a difference? Whether or not it is "difficult to interpret" becomes irrelevant from a scientific standpoint. A difference in statistics is just that: a difference.

The US military, for many years, did what they call an "exhaustive" investigation into the topic and attempted to track down all those military servicemembers that were involved in the experiments. There are many online resources, buried within dated websites and broken links, on the massive military network of websites. If you search hard enough, there are facts sheets and "frequently asked questions" regarding the programs, to show transparency and a willingness to assist those who feel they were negatively affected by the testing. However, the Government Accountability Office (GAO) did not feel that there was an adequate effort nor was the task at hand completed properly. In February of 2008, the independent, nonpartisan agency that works for Congress issued a report entitled, "Chemical and Biological Defense: DOD and VA Need to Improve Efforts to Identify and Notify Individuals Potentially Exposed during Chemical and Biological Tests." The conclusion of this particular report stated the following:

> Since World War II, potentially tens of thousands of military personnel and civilians have been exposed to chemical or biological substances during

previously classified DOD tests. As this population becomes older, it will become more imperative for DOD and VA to identify and notify these individuals in a timely manner because they might be eligible for health care or other benefits. While DOD has concluded that continuing an active search for individuals potentially exposed during Project 112 has reached a point of diminishing returns, it has not conducted an informed cost benefit analysis, which could guide DOD in identifying the extent to which it might need to take additional actions. Without conducting a sound and documented cost-benefit analysis that includes a full accounting of information known and the challenges associated with continuing to search for Project 112 participants, DOD will not be in a position to make an informed and transparent decision about whether any of the remaining investigative leads could result in meaningful opportunities to identify additional potentially exposed individuals. Furthermore, until DOD conducts such an analysis, Congress, veterans, and the public may continue to question the completeness and accuracy of DOD's efforts. Moreover, while DOD has undertaken efforts to identify and notify individuals who were potentially exposed during tests outside of Project 112, the department has not worked with veterans and veterans service organizations during its current effort as required by the Defense Authorization Act for FY 2003, and it has not coordinated its efforts with other DOD and non-DOD organizations. Until DOD and VA undertake more effective and efficient efforts to identify and notify potentially exposed individuals—including consistent guidance about the scope of work, such as clearly defined goals and objectives and agreement on the type and amount of information that is necessary to collect; effective internal controls and oversight practices; coordination with other entities to leverage existing information; regular updates to VA; and utilization of all available resources—Congress, veterans, and the public may continue to question DOD and VA's commitment to this effort. Furthermore, in the absence of transparency about these previously classified tests and DOD's efforts to identify individuals who were potentially exposed, Congress, veterans, and the public could have reason to believe that the cloak of secrecy has not been lifted and may not understand the success and challenges of DOD's current effort. While DOD and VA have developed a process for notifying servicemembers who were potentially exposed, it is unclear whether DOD or any other agency, such as the Department of Labor, is required to notify potentially exposed civilians who are identified. Therefore, without specific guidance that defines the requirements, roles and responsibilities, and mechanisms to notify civilians who have been potentially exposed to chemical or biological substances, these individuals might continue to be unaware of their circumstances.

In 2016, Congress mandated that the National Academy of Sciences do another study, as a follow-up to their 2007 report. With nearly another decade that passed since their original research, it proved to be an even bigger challenge to understand if those military personnel involved in Projects 112 and SHAD were affected by the testing. However, they produced another nearly two-hundred-page report. The conclusion stated:

> Epidemiological studies such as this investigation of health outcomes among veterans of the SHAD tests are complex undertakings requiring substantial time and resources. The committee invested considerable effort in learning about the SHAD tests and in formulating its approaches to data analysis. In the numerous analyses of both the full study population and of several subgroups, the only finding of a seemingly higher risk—of heart disease mortality among the 356 men who served on the USS *George Eastman*—did not attain statistical significance after adjustments for the multiple tests carried out on this group. The vast majority of the analyses showed no evidence of different health outcomes among SHAD veterans relative to the comparison group. The committee recognizes that with the limitations of epidemiological studies these negative findings cannot unequivocally rule out some potential effect from the SHAD testing. However, within the limits of the data available to the committee, the results of the analyses provide no evidence that the health of SHAD veterans overall or those in the exposure groups is significantly different from that of similar veterans who did not participate in these tests.

Yet again, the study repeated the finding of a "high risk" of heart disease, but immediately downplayed it by stating it was unable to attain a "statistical significance." It seems apparent, after writing this chapter, that the US government and military, either purposely or not, makes it incredibly difficult to ascertain an outcome to this all. Repeatedly, you see multiple studies, studies verifying the previous studies, documents that remain classified despite congressional pressure for transparency, and so much more.

OPERATION RANCH HAND

An overwhelming and even frightening number of projects/experiments resulted in human exposure. Even when these operations did not directly involve testing on humans like others mentioned in this chapter, humans were exposed to toxic chemicals and substances that would be connected to health problems appearing years later.

One example of such an occurrence happened during the conflict in Vietnam. It was known as Operation Ranch Hand, and it began in 1962 and lasted until 1971. During this program over the skies of Vietnam, Operation Ranch Hand dumped an estimated ten to twenty million gallons of herbicides and defoliants over South Vietnam. The aim was to destroy the food supply of the Viet Cong and the thick foliage/vegetation growth that gave them cover in the jungle.

In one 1978 report entitled, "The Toxicology, Environmental Fate and Human Risk of Herbicide Orange and Its Associated Dioxin," prepared by

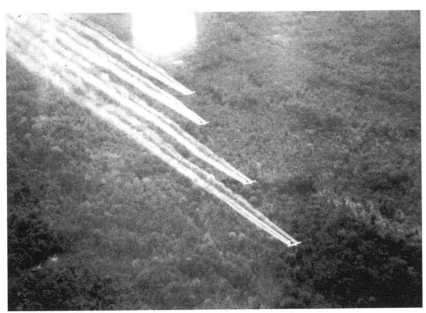

Figure 4.4. An official US Air Force photograph of a four-ship formation on a defoliation spray run during Operation Ranch Hand. *Credit*: US Air Force

the US Air Force Occupational and Environmental Health Laboratory at Brooks Air Force Base, the purpose of Operation Ranch Hand is explained:

> The introduction of herbicides in 1962 into the armed conflict in Vietnam represented an application of a new technique for modern warfare. Their use in a defensive role was for defoliation. Their use in offensive roles was for food crop denial. The herbicides most widely employed were the phenoxyacetic acids. They were extensively used for almost a decade throughout the forested, semi-populated, regions of South Vietnam.

The substances used during Operation Ranch Hand all had a color-coded system for naming, and collectively they were referred to as the "Rainbow Herbicides." These color designations resulted from the color of the barrel the herbicides were stored in, thus creating the naming system. For example, there were herbicides that were referred to as Agent White, Agent Blue, Agent Green, and Agent Pink. Yet, the most recognizable throughout the history books was Agent Orange.

In the 1990s, the Department of Veteran Affairs supported a study that later published a report entitled, "Veterans and Agent Orange: Health Effects of Herbicides Used in Vietnam." During this research study, Agent Orange, and its uses, were outlined in detail:

> Agent Orange, a 1:1 mixture of 2,4-D and the n-butyl ester of 2,4,5-T, accounted for approximately 61 percent of the recorded herbicide use. Orange was the general-purpose herbicide for defoliation and crop destruction, with leaf fall in three to six weeks and control persisting for seven to twelve months. According to military estimates of herbicide use, 90 percent of Agent Orange was used in Ranch Hand forest defoliation missions; 8 percent was used in Ranch Hand crop destruction missions; and 2 percent was sprayed from the ground around base perimeters and cache sites, waterways, and communication lines. Mangrove forests were especially sensitive to the effects of Agent Orange—a single application killed them. Annual crops were killed rapidly by one application of Agent Orange; root and tuber crops, and perennial and woody tropical crops such as jackfruit, papaya, and mango, were also susceptible to Agent Orange.
>
> Orange II was introduced later in the program. It differed from the original Agent Orange in that the n-butyl ester of 2,4,5-T was replaced by the isooctyl ester; however their herbicidal effects were similar. According to

procurement records, less than 10 percent of the total Agent Orange used was Orange II.

In other words, Agent Orange and the other "Rainbow Herbicides" were potent mixes of various chemicals and elements that would eventually cause health risks to those exposed. But the main issue after the health risks were discovered was finding those who may have been affected. The "Veterans and Agent Orange: Health Effects of Herbicides Used in Vietnam" report explains:

Although the number of US military personnel exposed to herbicides is impossible to determine precisely, the majority of those assigned to Operation Ranch Hand can be presumed to have been exposed to Agent Orange and other herbicides. During the entire operation, approximately 1,250 military personnel served in Ranch Hand units. Although the Air Force maintained complete records of its Operation Ranch Hand fixed-wing herbicide missions, documentation of spraying conducted on the ground by boat, truck, or backpack and authorized at the unit level was less systematic. Authorization for herbicide missions by helicopter or surface spraying from riverboats, trucks, and hand-operated backpacks was delegated to the Republic of Vietnam and US authorities at the Corps level; these operations required only the approval of the unit commanders or senior advisors. "Free-spraying" areas, including the Demilitarized Zone (DMZ) at the seventeenth parallel and the first 100 meters outside base camps, were also exempt from Ranch Hand regulations (NAS, 1974). This delegation of authority for spraying to the Corps level reduced the lag time that existed from proposal to completion of small defoliation projects, such as around depots, airfields, and outposts (Collins, 1967). However, because these helicopter and ground sprays were less rigidly controlled than fixed-wing aerial sprayings, the recording of such sprays was not as systematic as those of Operation Ranch Hand.

There have been many studies to determine the exact health effects of this exposure, and results vary. Though one thing is generally palpable: exposure to the "Rainbow Herbicides" was not good. A 2010 Congressional Research Service (CRS) report entitled, "Veterans Affairs: Health Care and Benefits for Veterans Exposed to Agent Orange," outlines just some of the diseases associated with exposure:

Currently, the conditions that are presumptively recognized for service connection for Vietnam veterans are chloracne (must occur within one year of exposure to Agent Orange); non-Hodgkin's lymphoma; soft tissue sarcoma (other than osteosarcoma, chondrosarcoma, Kaposi's sarcoma, or mesothelioma); Hodgkin's disease; porphyria cutanea tarda (must occur within one year of exposure); multiple myeloma; respiratory cancers, including cancers of the lung, larynx, trachea, and bronchus; prostate cancer; acute and subacute transient peripheral neuropathy (must appear within one year of exposure and resolve within two years of date of onset); type II diabetes; chronic lymphocytic leukemia (CLL); amyotrophic lateral sclerosis (ALS); and AL amyloidosis.

This same report also goes into the fact that despite the original stance by the Department of Defense (DOD) regarding Agent Orange exposure, they were forced to correct themselves.

Since the late 1970s, Vietnam-era veterans have voiced concerns about how exposure to Agent Orange may have affected their health and caused certain disabilities, including birth defects in their children. Initially, the Department of Defense (DOD) maintained that only a limited number of US military personnel, such as those operating aircraft or troops engaged in herbicide spraying, could be positively linked to Agent Orange exposure. However, in 1979, the General Accounting Office, now the Government Accountability Office (GAO), reported that ground troops had also been exposed to Agent Orange, and DOD was forced to reconsider its prior statements. In response to these concerns, Congress passed legislation to research the long-term health effects on Vietnam veterans and to provide benefits and services to those who may have been exposed to Agent Orange.

The biggest hindrance to researching these programs, despite the complexity and classification of the material, is simply the passage of time. Studies do not take weeks or months, but rather years to understand the full effects of such programs on those exposed. Not only with those exposed to Agent Orange, but also those who were unknowingly the test subjects of an untold number of experiments, projects, and programs that used "harmless" substances.

Figure 4.5. Agent Orange was transported in barrels with a single orange band. This color-coding of barrels gave the various "Rainbow Herbicides" their nicknames. *Credit*: US Air Force

Thorough, but time-consuming studies do offer detailed results that can be established and used as a reference for offering the groundwork to proper compensation to those involved. However, the real result from this long, drawn-out process, is literally an entire generation of people, including those involved in the tests, that will die off. Interest in the details will be lost, and those researchers who are wholeheartedly interested in the truth will cease to exist. Maybe that's the plan.

II

BEYOND THE
IRON CURTAIN

5

AMERICA AND THE SOVIET UNION INHERIT THE NAZIS

From about 1947 through approximately 1991 (there are differing views on when exactly the Cold War began and ended), there was a massive amount of tension between the Soviet Union and the United States that began just after World War II. This period between the two nations is referred to as the Cold War. After Nazi Germany fell and Imperial Japan surrendered, America and the Soviet Union found themselves at a crossroads. The geopolitical tension between the two nations saw communism face off with democracy in a "war" that would last for decades.

During the Cold War, there were countless incidents, projects, and programs during America's "fight" with the Soviet Union, all of which did not involve firing bullets or dropping bombs on each other. This part of Cold War history has remained very far from the public eye and behind a curtain of secrecy for decades. But how did this war even start?

During World War II, the Soviet Union and United States found themselves struggling between ideological, geopolitical, and economic issues. Both countries aimed to be at the top, yet they found themselves forcibly united to fight the Nazi regime in Europe. During this period, tensions would rise as democracy was forced to work side by side with communism. However, that romance would not last for long.

NAZI SUPERIORITY

The United States stormed Europe from the west, and the Soviet Union came in from the East in order to sandwich Nazi Germany in the middle until the fall of Berlin. Yet, along the way, both nations were seizing as much intelligence as they could gather, as they plowed across Europe. Both nations knew, as they were fighting it firsthand, that Nazi science and technology was on the cutting edge. Hitler's Germany had made advancements that no other nation had made, and they had weapons like the V-1 and V-2 rockets that were more powerful than any other nation was wielding in battle at the time. This type of intelligence was paramount to getting the upper hand post-war, and both America and the Soviet Union were trying to capitalize on whatever they could find, wherever they could find it. Arguably, the intelligence that sprouted out of one location, Peenemunde, would forever shape the coming "Cold War."

Peenemunde was instrumental for Nazi Germany in the development of rockets like the V-1 and V-2. The National Museum of the US Air Force describes Peenemunde:

Figure 5.1.   Cutaway drawing of the V-2 showing engine, fuel cells, guidance units, and warhead. *Credit*: US Air Force

The V-1 and V-2 were developed at Peenemunde, on the island of Usedom on Germany's Baltic Sea coast. The Luftwaffe and German army shared this research site, which was ideally suited to secret rocket and flying bomb testing because it was isolated, flat, and had plenty of room for flight testing without endangering inhabited areas. In the summer of 1943, Allied reconnaissance discovered rockets at Peenemunde. Soon after, bombing raids slowed German work there and forced them to move manufacturing elsewhere.

The intelligence that could be gathered at places like Peenemunde, which included papers, schematics, and drawings, would undoubtedly progress the respective nations that would capture it. The Soviet Union and the United States both knew this, and as they were racking up the various major victories on the battlefield, both nations would ensure that no viable intelligence would be left in their wake.

Yet, it was not only the document intelligence that would prove invaluable; it was also the people. Scientists who played crucial roles in the development of rockets, weapons, and even battle plans for the Nazis would all be valuable prisoners to their captors. One of those valuable human commodities would be the leader of the V-2 rocket program for the Nazis: Major-General Walter Dornberger, who worked at Peenemunde.

In one declassified document entitled, "An Air Force History of Space Activities, 1945–1959," written by the US Air Force Historical Division Liaison Office in August 1964, it describes the effort of intelligence gathering for the Allied superpowers:

> The collapse of Peenemuende began soon after the launching of the V-2 offensive. By autumn 1944 the war was sweeping toward the Nazi defeat. The Russians raced through eastern Germany and in January 1945 threatened Peenemuende. In the confusion of disaster, Dornberger could not save his entire group, and a number of his employees, some with 10 years experience, had no choice but to remain at the experimental station. A small section that fortunately included Dornberger and some of his most highly qualified specialists escaped westward to the Harts Mountains. They took with them invaluable papers and established a new installation that functioned only in the sense of holding together scientists who might otherwise have been scattered and lost.
>
> In the spring of 1945 the Russians occupied Peenemuende. They transported to Russia 4,000 scientists and workers along with most of the equip-

ment, production facilities, and as many documents as they could find. Inside the Soviet Union the Russians reconstituted Peenemuende in a diminished version and operated it as a rocket research center. The captured Germans manufactured new models of the V-2 and in this way between 1946 and 1948 supplied the Russians with missiles for at least 500 experimental firings. By that time, the Soviets felt they had drained the Germans of all possible

Figure 5.2.   The head of the V-2 rocket program at Peenemunde, Major-General Walter Dornberger. *Credit*: Bundesarchiv, Bild 146-1980-009-33 / CC-BY-SA 3.0

contributory knowledge and, after a long period of isolation, permitted their prisoners to return home. The Germans remained ignorant of the Russian competence in the field of missile propulsion and knew nothing of the Russian overall rocket program.

When the Americans overran the Harts Mountains in May 1945, they found quantities of the Peenemuende records and, even more important, some of the men responsible for the work. At once the US Army seized the documents, blueprints and data and shipped them to the United States. Soon afterwards the Army initiated Operation Paperclip and brought to the United States 180 of the scientists who had played leading roles at Peenemuende.

OPERATION PAPERCLIP

Operation Paperclip became a crucial part of American history in its role in the "space race" that would later begin with the Soviet Union. Major-General Dornberger, who had fled from Peenemunde, was not present when the Soviets captured the rocket facility on May 5, 1945. For the Americans, and arguably the world, that was a good thing.

His background, knowledge, and expertise would surely have benefited them; however, that never happened. He, along with the chief scientist of the rocket group at Peenemunde, later surrendered to the US Seventh Army that same month. The scientist's name that surrendered to the Americans with Major-General Dornberger: Dr. Wernher von Braun.

The Good

Under Operation Paperclip, both men (along with many others) found their way to the United States to work for the Americans. There, they would share their knowledge of rockets and advanced propulsion engines. Though, it was not only the United States that had a program to import Nazi scientists. The Soviet Union also had initiated Operation Osoaviakhim, wherein they literally removed approximately 2,200 German specialists from Soviet-occupied zones. Adding in family members, the total forcibly removed was estimated at more than 6,000—and the Russians did it all in a single night.

Although the Soviet Union was much more forceful than the United States during this acquisition, the intelligence shared by former Nazi scientists and specialists would quickly be utilized to make weapon systems and rocket technology bigger and more advanced. However, both nations utilized the intelligence they gathered in different ways.

The document "An Air Force History of Space Activities, 1945–1959" explains:

> Having thus scavenged the broken body of Peenemuende, the Russians and Americans reacted very differently to the taste of their spoils. The Soviet government understood that rockets would be of paramount important in the future and directed their nascent program toward nothing more definite, and nothing less inclusive, than the advancement of rocket science regardless of its specific applicability. The result was that by 1956 or 1957 the Russians had a rocket engine—or possibly rocket engines—with a thrust that could launch either missiles laden with atomic warheads or heavily instrumented capsules to orbit the earth or explore interplanetary space. The Americans, in contrast, had little top-level guidance or support and they fragmented their development of rocket engines among a number of projects within a comprehensive but frequently unstable missile program. The unfortunate consequence was that in 1956 and 1957 the United States had no rocket propulsion comparable to that enjoyed by the Soviet Union.

With that, the "space race" was on. Both the United States and Russia wanted to conquer space and, eventually, land a man on the moon, no matter the cost. Conquering this frontier would mean strategic advances both scientifically and militaristically, and both nations began feverishly working to beat the other to the finish line.

In the 1960s, when the "space race" entered the period of its quickest pace, one facility that played a crucial role in rocket development for America was the Air Force Special Weapons Center (AFSWC). The AFSWC was based at Kirtland Air Force Base, New Mexico, from 1949 through 1976. It first operated as the Special Weapons Command (SWC) and then, in 1952, was renamed to the AFSWC, where it operated until 1976. According to a document released by the US Air Force, part of the "Air Force Nuclear Weapons Center History," the AFSWC was described as the following:

> The Air Force redesignated Special Weapons Command as the Air Force Special Weapons Center on 1 April 1952, and was assigned to the newly activated Air Research and Development Command. During the 1950s, Air

Force Special Weapons Center personnel and aircraft participated in atmospheric nuclear tests in Nevada and the far Pacific. On July 1, 1952, Indian Springs (today Creech) Air Force Base, Nevada, was transferred to the control of the Air Force Special Weapons Center.

By the mid-1950s, the Air Force had established a large scientific and technical presence at Kirtland Air Force Base such as biophysicists who deliberately flew through nuclear clouds to determine radiation hazards and engineers who launched sounding rockets to study the effects of high-altitude explosions and physicists who studied the nature of the recently discovered Van Allen radiation belts around the Earth.

In 1958 Air Force Special Weapons Center scientists began to simulate the effects of explosions in order to strengthen missiles, missile sites, and aircraft against possible attack. The Air Force Weapons Laboratory at Kirtland Air Force Base was created from elements of the Special Weapons Center Research Directorate in 1963 and thus the Special Weapons Center gave up much of its research and development work. The Air Force Special Weapons Center continued however with its test and evaluation mission and as Kirtland's host organization.

The Air Force Special Weapons Center assumed management of Air Force Systems Command's test and evaluation facilities at Holloman Air Force Base, New Mexico, during the summer of 1970.

The AFSWC would go through various names through the decades, eventually landing on the Air Force Nuclear Weapons Center (AFNWC) in March of 2006. Yet, it was this highly secretive history through the 1950s and 1960s that led to the development of highly advanced rocket delivery systems. According to the "National Register of Historic Places Historic Context and Evaluation for Kirtland Air Force Base," published in June 2003, it was clear how crucial the role was of those scientists and specialists that came from Nazi Germany to the advancement of various programs:

> Throughout the remainder of the 1960s, the AFSWC worked closely with the Air Force Missile Development Center at Holloman AFB. The AFSWC's responsibilities at this time included the testing and evaluation of airborne missiles, aircraft reconnaissance systems, and missile reentry vehicles (KAFB 1971). The precursor to the Air Force Missile Development Center was the Guided Missile Test Range, which was established at the Alamogordo Army Air Field (AAF) in 1947 to develop and test pilotless aircraft, guided missiles,

and the associated systems and equipment (Lewis et al. 1997). Many of the facilities and personnel from Wendover Army Air Base (AAB) were transferred to Alamogordo AAF [renamed Holloman AFB in 1948] to develop the test range (Lewis et al. 1997).

Many of the scientists that participated in the early missile program at Holloman AFB came from Operation Paperclip, which was designed to ensure scientific and military superiority and was one of the earliest manifestations of the Cold War arms race. At the end of World War II, the US and Soviet Union fiercely competed for the German Peenemünde rocket scientists who had excelled at military technological developments over the previous two decades. Through Operation Paperclip the US identified, recruited, and brought German scientists and technologists to the US to aid in the development of American military missiles (Lewis et al. 1997).

The early work of the Operation Paperclip scientists at Holloman AFB involved the German V-2 rocket. Throughout the Cold War, the Air Force Missile Development Center launched many missiles, including Tiny Tim (the first US Army rocket), Rascal, XQ-2 Drone, Falcon, MACE, Matador, and Shrike (Holloman n.d.). By the late 1950s more German scientists and engineers had worked at Holloman AFB (approximately 70) than at any other USAF installation, with the exception of Wright-Patterson AFB (Weitze 2001).

The scientists and specialists that came into the United States through Operation Paperclip played various roles through many corners of scientific research. The most recognizable name that came out of the program, who was already mentioned as surrendering with Major-General Dornberger, was von Braun. As someone who helped design the V-2 rocket for the Nazis, von Braun's expertise would be utilized for the Americans to create the rockets that took the first satellite for the United States into space—the Explorer 1.

However, he was far from the only influential scientist. Another would be Kurt Heinrich Debus, who also worked on the V-2 rocket program for the Nazis. He, too, would be brought over through Operation Paperclip, and he would move up the ranks to become the first director of NASA's Launch Operations Center, which we know today as the Kennedy Space Center. He would hold that position from 1962 through 1974.

Figure 5.3. After arriving at the Cape Canaveral Missile Test Annex Skid Strip on September 11, 1962, President John F. Kennedy is welcomed by a color guard and Center Director Kurt Debus (right). *Credit*: **NASA**

Debus would, in many cases, have face-to-face interactions with President John F. Kennedy during the race to the moon. He is highly revered in the history of the space program, as NASA highlights in a 2007 article published about Debus:

Born in Frankfurt, Germany, in 1908, Debus' education and rocketry experience in his home country landed him in the post–World War II ballistic missile systems development program in the US. He and about 100 German colleagues, led by rocket pioneer Wernher von Braun, worked first at Fort Bliss, Texas, before relocating to Huntsville, Ala. Their work became the focal point of the Army's rocket and space projects and Cape Canaveral became their launch site.

Debus came to the Cape in the early 1950s to set up a launch site, and permanently moved to the area with his family by the middle of the decade. By 1960, the Army Ballistic Missile Agency was transferred to the National Aeronautics and Space Administration. On July 1, 1962, the Florida launch facility at Cape Canaveral was officially designated as NASA's Launch Operations Center (it was renamed to honor the fallen president just after his assassination in 1963) and Debus was officially named its first center director.

By that time, construction of the spaceport under Debus' leadership was well under way. While the space hardware was under development, physical structures like the launchpads and the Vehicle Assembly Building rose on what had been coastal wilderness.

Amid the flurry of building facilities and developing rockets that would take men into orbit and on to the moon, Debus had the forethought to consider the natural environment that surrounded the center. He arranged for the US Department of the Interior to establish and maintain a wildlife refuge at the space center. Thanks to his efforts, the 140,000-acre Merritt Island National Wildlife Refuge exists today.

With growing pride and enthusiasm on the part of the public toward the space program, Debus secured support for the first visitor center, as well.

By the time Debus retired as center director in 1974, the list of human space achievements under his leadership represents some of the greatest in US history. Among them:

- 1961—Alan Shepard Jr. became the first American in space
- 1962—John Glenn Jr. became the first American to orbit Earth
- 1969—The Apollo program's first lunar landing; Neil Armstrong was the first man on the moon
- 1973—Skylab, a science and engineering laboratory, was launched into Earth orbit

The Bad

However, Operation Paperclip did not always have such a glowing outcome from their recruits like they did with von Braun and with Debus. For example, one engineer who was brought over under Operation Paperclip, who was also heavily involved in the development of the V-2, was Georg Johannes Rickhey. He was taken by the US Army to work at, and live, within Wright-Patterson Air Force Base, but was indicted as part of the Dachau Trials in 1947. He was accused of working closely with the SS and the Gestapo and having witnessed multiple executions. Although acquitted due to a lack of evidence, he would never return to his work within the United States.

Another was Dr. Walter Schreiber, who came to the United States in 1952 also through Operation Paperclip. Dr. Schreiber was a German medical military officer who was captured by the Soviet Red Army in April of 1945. He was taken to the Soviet Union, where he later appeared as a wit-

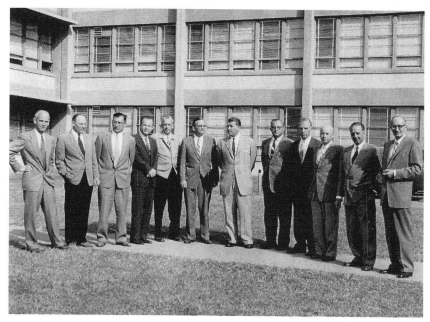

Figure 5.4.   Twelve scientific specialists of the Peenemunde team stand at the front of Building 4488, Redstone Arsenal, Huntsville, Alabama. They led the army's space efforts at ABMA before the team transferred to the National Aeronautics and Space Administration's George C. Marshall Space Flight Center. (Left to right) Dr. Ernst Stuhlinger, Dr. Helmut Hoelzer, Karl L. Heimburg, Dr. Ernst Geissler, Erich W. Neubert, Dr. Walter Haeussermann, Dr. Wernher von Braun, William A. Mrazek, Hans Hueter, Eberhard Rees, Dr. Kurt Debus, and Hans H. Maus. *Credit*: Courtesy of NASA Marshall Space Flight Center

ness in the Nuremberg Trials, where he gave evidence against Hermann Goring and Kurt Blome, the man in charge of the Nazi's biological weapons development program. It was this testimony that would come back to haunt him years later.

After Dr. Schreiber escaped from his Soviet handler in 1948, he fled to Berlin and surrendered to the Allied Control Authority that served, at the time, as the governing body over Germany and Austria. Although the Allied Control Authority consisted of members from the Soviet Union, the United States, the United Kingdom, and France, Dr. Schreiber was hired to work with the Counter Intelligence Corps, an intelligence arm of the US Army. He later would find his way to America and work within the Air Force School of Medicine at Randolph Air Force Base, Texas. In the early 1950s, controversy would erupt when the public learned about Dr. Schreiber and his employment by the US military. On February 14, 1952, the *Free Lance-Star* issued the gruesome details behind the Nazi doctor:

Air Force Hires Nazi Doctor Linked to Ghastly Experiments

WASHINGTON—Here are the facts regarding the Nazi doctor who escaped the Nuremberg war crimes trials and is now working for the Air Force at Randolph Field, Texas. He is Dr. Walter P. Schreiber, the Wehrmacht's wartime chief of medical science, who sanctioned some of the ghastly medical experiments which the Nazis performed on hopeless victims.

The reason Scheirber [sic] wasn't tried as a war criminal was that he mysteriously disappeared until the deadline for indictment had passed. When finally he came out of hiding, he was given a job by the Air Force instead of being tried for war crimes. Today he is working on a secret research project at the Air Force School of Aviation Medicine, Randolph Field, Texas.

The article then went on to list four major war crimes and human atrocities that Dr. Schreiber committed. The details are gruesome but include the following. I spared my readers the nitty-gritty details, for obvious reasons.

1. Tests that involve the injection of phenol (a substance that causes chemical burns) into the arms of humans. At least four prisoners at the Buchenwald concentration camp were involved in the tests as ordered by Dr. Schreiber, wherein humans were forcefully injected with the phenol. All died as a result, and the Nazis considered the experiments a success.

2. Young Polish girls were held down by SS troops and operated on at the Ravensbrueck concentration camp, which resulted in gas gangrene. At least three girls were killed in this forced surgical environment, and it is believed based on the testimony of Dr. Karl Gebhardt before he was executed for war crimes, that Dr. Schreiber had received reports and updates on these experiments and showed no objection.

3. At the Buchenwald and Natzweiler concentration camps, typhus was passed back and forth between mice and human guinea pigs at the camp, with the intent to create a live vaccine. Many of the test subjects, both animal and human, were killed during the experiments. Professor Eugene Haagen, who conducted the experiments at both

camps, wrote to ask Dr. Schreiber for additional mice for use with the experiments, though he was stocked on the human subjects since both camps could be utilized. Dr. Schreiber had affirmed the request, and in his response letter dated June 20, 1944, it was evident that he was fully aware of the horrific experiments.

4. Multiple experiments were conducted by throwing humans into tubs of ice-cold water to study the shock reactions by the body. It is unclear how many test subjects perished during these tests, however, Dr. Schreiber's name was on a restricted list of those being updated on the developments.

These horrific war crimes that Dr. Schreiber escaped being tried for offer a glimpse at some of the people brought over through Operation Paperclip. Of course, we cannot say all who were brought over played a role in such horrific experiments, but what is bothersome is the fact that Dr. Schreiber, after investigation by American authorities, was "cleared" to work for the US Air Force. Why was the evidence of his background missed, or overlooked?

After news broke about Dr. Schreiber's past and his employment by the US Air Force, he was forced into hiding. After his contract with the US Air Force was not renewed, he temporarily moved to California to be with one of his daughters, but was then given money by the US military, along with being handed a visa, and flown by military transport to New Orleans in May of 1952. There, he boarded another plane and lived the rest of his days, with a second daughter, in Buenos Aires, Argentina.

Despite the fleeing of Dr. Schreiber, many of those who came to the United States under Operation Paperclip would stay, work, and be promoted. They would play an instrumental role in launching the first satellite orbiting the Earth and later putting a man on the moon.

With such an eclectic background to the scientists involved in the "space race," it should come as no surprise that the public was not given the whole story. Television nightly news broadcasts would tell one story about the race to set foot on the moon. Yet behind the scenes, a completely different, and classified, picture would begin to emerge.

6

INCHES FROM
NUCLEAR WAR

To most who study world history, politics, and military conflict, there is nothing more frightening than nuclear warfare. According to "Global Nuclear Weapons Inventories, 1945–2010" by Robert S. Norris and Hans M. Kristensen, the Soviet Union and the United States had reached nearly seventy thousand nuclear weapons in their inventories by the mid-1980s.

After the bombing of Hiroshima and Nagasaki by the United States in August of 1945, which led to the surrender of Japan and thus ending World War II, the threat of nuclear war has loomed. The nuclear weapons dropped on those two cities showed the world that whomever possessed such inventory would undoubtedly have an upper hand in any battle.

So, when the Cold War escalated, both the United States and the Soviet Union knew that they needed to have a larger quantity of weapons that were bigger and more powerful than the other. As each year passed, their inventories would increase in size and destructive magnitude, all while the threat of nuclear war between the two nations grew closer.

On October 30, 1961, the Soviet Union detonated the largest atomic bomb to date, known as Tsar Bomba. It was a fifty-megaton behemoth, which according to the Defense Threat Reduction Agency (DTRA), a branch of the Department of Defense (DOD) that offers combat support to American armed forces, held the destructive power of more than ten times of *all* the explosives used in World War II *combined*. To put it another way, it's calculated that the Tsar Bomba blast was more than fifteen hundred times the combined energy of both the bombs that destroyed Nagasaki and Hiroshima. In other words, this thing was big!

Around the same time as the Soviet Union detonated the world's largest nuclear bomb in the 1960s, the United States developed what they called the "nuclear triad." This referred to three delivery mechanisms for nuclear weapons: land-based intercontinental ballistic missiles, submarine-launched ballistic missiles, and strategic aerial bombers with nuclear capability. This ensured that should a nuclear war break out, another nation could not destroy America's capability of delivering such weapons in one single strike. The "nuclear triad" allowed the United States continuity to function for retaliatory strikes, since they had mastered land, sea, and air delivery mechanisms. If all air delivery systems were destroyed, then land-based intercontinental ballistic missiles could be launched; if all land area was destroyed that housed nuclear launch silos, then sea-based delivery systems could launch, and so on.

In 2015, the Chief Historian for the Defense Logistics Agency (DLA), Harold Raugh, published an article about the history of the "nuclear triad," and he had this to say about the Cold War era and the threat of nuclear war:

> This US-Soviet nuclear arms race resulted in a situation of mutual deterrence in the 1960s. The size and capabilities of the superpowers' nuclear arsenals, if employed, had the potential to produce mutually assured destruction, which forced restraint on both sides.
>
> This nuclear stalemate also served as the genesis for the US nuclear triad. In addition to permitting each of the US military services to play a role in nuclear deterrence, the three different nuclear basing and delivery modes had complementary strengths and weaknesses. As noted by Amy W. Woolf in a 2015 Congressional Research Service study on US nuclear forces, "ICBMs eventually had the accuracy and prompt responsiveness needed to attack hardened targets such as Soviet command posts and ICBM silos, [and] SLBMs had the survivability needed to complicate Soviet efforts to launch a disarming first strike and to retaliate if such an attack were attempted." The third component of the nuclear triad, strategic bombers, "could be dispersed quickly and launched to enhance their survivability, and they could be recalled to their bases if a crisis did not escalate into conflict."
>
> The number of nuclear delivery vehicles—ICBMs, SLBMs and nuclear-capable bombers—in the US force structure, according to unclassified es-

timates compiled by Woolf, grew steadily through the mid-1960s, peaking at 2,268 in 1967. Between 1,875 and 2,200 ICBMs, SLBMs and heavy bombers were generally maintained through 1990. The number of warheads remained steady before peaking at 13,600 in 1987.

With power like that, a nuclear war would not only destroy any nation that took part in it, but it would quite possibly eliminate humanity off the face of the Earth from the fallout and other long-term consequences. There-fore, both nations worked hard to arm themselves, but they also tried to ensure that none of this happened. Should a nuclear holocaust break out, it was theorized that there would be no decisive "winner" in such a conflict, so it was avoided at all costs.

However, what would happen if nuclear war was triggered—by accident? Declassified documents reveal that it happened on more than one occasion, and the world came closer to the brink than was ever known at the time.

NUCLEAR FALSE ALARM—SEPTEMBER 1983

On September 26, 1983, five intercontinental ballistic missiles launched by the United States were detected by Russian early warning systems. One, according to the instrumentation utilized by the Russians, was heading di-rectly toward the capital of the Soviet Union—Moscow.

The detection was made within the Serpukhov-15 bunker located near the Russian capital, and it served as the command center for Soviet early warning satellites used to spot nuclear launches. Upon detection of the five warheads, a lieutenant colonel in the Soviet Air Defense Forces, Stanislav Petrov, had a decision to make that would forever alter world history.

Issue #1349 of the "United States Air Force—Center for Strategic Deter-rence Studies—News and Analysis," dated January 18, 2019, recounts the incident:

On 26 September 1983, Stanislav Petrov was the duty officer at the Soviet early warning system command. Soviet satellites detected the launch of a US first strike, and the reliability of the report was rated as "Highest." In this situ-ation, Petrov's standing orders required him to report the alert up the chain of command. In 1983, the Soviet leadership was extremely worried about the possibility of a US first strike. It is therefore likely that, if Petrov had reported the alarm (of the highest reliability) to his superiors, the Soviets would have followed their doctrine and retaliated. Petrov's gut instinct was telling him that the alarm was false. Fortunately for the world, Petrov ignored his orders and went with his gut instinct.

A 2011 document authored by the Center for Strategic and Budgetary Assessments entitled, "How to Think about Nuclear Forces and Deterrence in the 21st Century," explained what ultimately happened that caused the false alarm:

it was later determined that a rare alignment of sunlight off high-altitude clouds and the satellite's Molniya orbits had generated the false missile tracks, which an associated computer program had failed to filter out.

The incident came amid high tensions and concerns that nuclear war was inevitable. Should Petrov have reported the incident, nuclear war would undoubtedly have occurred within minutes. The only thing that stopped him from doing so was that Petrov's gut instinct told him that America firing five missiles made no strategic sense. America would rather, in his opinion, fire a large number of warheads should a "first strike" occur. This ensured massive destruction of the Soviet Union and would surely destroy all means of retaliation by destroying Russian launch sites.

CIA historian Ben Fischer wrote a "Secret" article entitled, "The 1983 War Scare in US-Soviet Relations," which was originally published in the CIA's "Studies in Intelligence" journal. In it, Fischer outlines the aura of 1983 and relations with the Soviet Union, leading up to Petrov's world-altering decision:

On 23 March 1983, President Reagan announced a program to develop a ground- and space-based, laser-armed, anti-ballistic-missile shield designated Strategic Defense Initiative (SDI) but quickly dubbed "Star Wars" by the media. Four days later—and in direct response—[Yuri] Andropov [sixth leader of the Soviet Union] lashed out. He accused the United States of preparing a first-strike attack on the USSR and asserted that Reagan was "inventing new plans on how to unleash a nuclear war in the best way, with the hope of winning it."

Andropov's remarks were unprecedented. He violated a long-standing taboo by describing US nuclear weapons' numbers and capabilities in the

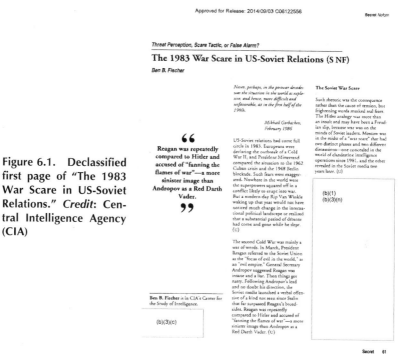

Figure 6.1. Declassified first page of "The 1983 War Scare in US-Soviet Relations." *Credit*: Central Intelligence Agency (CIA)

mass media. He referred to Soviet weapons and capabilities—also highly unusual—and said explicitly that the USSR had, at best, only parity with the United States in strategic weaponry. And, for the first time since 1953, a Soviet leader was telling the Soviet people that the world was on the verge of a nuclear holocaust. If candor is a sign of sincerity, Moscow was worried.

This document certainly sheds light on the emotions at the time. This high tension, on both sides, would play a role in the months and years to come that would bring the world to the brink of nuclear annihilation.

ABLE ARCHER 83—NOVEMBER 1983

In 1983, an exercise known as "Able Archer" took place by the North Atlantic Treaty Organization (NATO). NATO, which is also referred to as the "North Atlantic Alliance," is an intergovernmental military group of

American and European nations. It began on April 4, 1949, and the party members of the group all agree to a mutual defense of each other should a major battle break out.

As a result, periodic operations and exercises take place to train for such a scenario, like "Able Archer." The exercise would occur annually, and "Able Archer" would allow all participating nations to practice command and control procedures during a time of war.

In a released entry from the "Intellipedia" system, a data-sharing website used by the US Intelligence Community (IC), "Able Archer" and the subsequent exercise in 1983 known as "Able Archer 83" was described as the following:

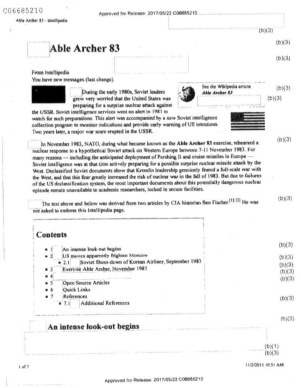

Figure 6.2. One of the released pages from Intellipedia, which outlines Able Archer 83. *Credit*: National Security Agency (NSA)

During the early 1980s, Soviet leaders grew very worried that the United States was preparing for a surprise nuclear attack against the USSR. Soviet intelligence services went on alert in 1981 to watch for such preparations. This alert was accompanied by a new Soviet intelligence collection program to monitor indications and provide early warning of US intentions. Two years later, a major war scare erupted in the USSR.

In November 1983, NATO, during what became known as the Able Archer 83 exercise, rehearsed a nuclear response to a hypothetical Soviet attack on Western Europe between 7–11 November 1983. For many reasons—including the anticipated deployment of Pershing II and cruise missiles in Europe—Soviet intelligence was at that time actively preparing for a possible surprise nuclear missile attack by the West. Declassified Soviet documents show that Kremlin leadership genuinely feared a full-scale war with the West, and that this fear greatly increased the risk of nuclear war in the fall of 1983. But due to failures of the US declassification system, the most important documents about this potentially dangerous nuclear episode remain unavailable to academic researchers, locked in secure facilities.

The text above and below was derived from two articles by CIA historian Ben Fischer. He was asked to endorse this Intellipedia page.

The Intellipedia system is an immensely powerful took utilized by the IC. Within it are literally millions of pages (which was unknown for many years until a FOIA appeal was won by The Black Vault that revealed the statistics) that deal with countless topics. With three systems that comprise Intellipedia, including a Top Secret, Secret, and Unclassified version, these millions of entries can reveal an amazing amount of what I call "FOIA fodder," wherein you can find leads to other documents and material to request.

This entry is a prime example. Let me point you to one of the most intriguing lines within the Intellipedia entry again: "But due to failures of the US declassification system, the most important documents about this potentially dangerous nuclear episode remain unavailable to academic researchers, locked in secure facilities." Is a CIA history eluding to a cover-up here? The last line I quoted about pointed me in the direction of where I might find the answer to that. I tracked down one of Fischer's articles (the other referenced was classified), and it helped shed more light on "Able Archer 83."

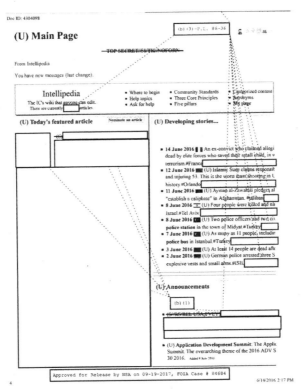

Figure 6.3. A declassified main page for the "Top Secret" version of Intellipedia. *Credit*: National Security Agency (NSA)

Another notable incident in 1983 occurred during an annual NATO command post exercise codenamed ABLE ARCHER 83. The Soviets were familiar with this exercise from previous years, but the 1983 version included two important changes:

- In the original scenario (which was later modified), the 1983 exercise was to involve high-level officials, including the Secretary of Defense and the Chairman of the Joint Chiefs of Staff in major roles, with cameo appearances by the President and the Vice President. Such high-level participation would have meant greater publicity and visibility than was the case during past runnings of this exercise.
- ABLE ARCHER 83 included a practice drill that took NATO forces through a full-scale simulated release of nuclear weapons.

According to [Oleg] Gordievsky [former colonel of the KGB, who later defected to the United States], on the night of November 8 or 9—he was not sure which—the KGB Center sent a flash cable to West European residencies advising them, incorrectly, that US forces in Europe had gone on alert and that troops at some bases were being mobilized. The cable speculated that the (nonexistent) alert might have been ordered in response to the then-recent bomb attack on the US Marine barracks in Lebanon, or was related to impending US Army maneuvers, or was the beginning of a countdown to a surprise nuclear attack. Recipients were asked to confirm the US alert and evaluate these hypotheses.

Gordievsky described the reaction in stark terms:

> In the tense atmosphere generated by the crises and rhetoric of the past few months, the KGB concluded that American forces had been placed on alert—and might even have begun the countdown to war. . . . The world did not quite reach the edge of the nuclear abyss during Operation RYAN. But during ABLE ARCHER 83 it had, without realizing it, come frighteningly close—certainly closer than at any time since the Cuban missile crisis of 1962.

The article by CIA historian Fischer went on to question whether or not Gordievsky's recollection of "Able Archer" was embellished, as it compared the scare to having come closer than any moment of the Cuban missile crisis in 1962. Despite some records being hidden or possibly even destroyed, as they are scarce, the Intellipedia entry also added some points that it was not just "Able Archer 83" that spooked the Soviets, but rather, it was a progression of incidents that seemingly played a role in bringing to world to the brink of nuclear war.

> Moscow's new sense of urgency was explicitly linked to the impending deployment of US Pershing II intermediate-range ballistic missiles in West Germany. The Soviets, as well as some Western military experts, saw the Pershings as a new, destabilizing element in the nuclear balance. The missiles were highly accurate and able to destroy Soviet hard targets, including command-and-control bunkers and missile silos. Their flight time from Germany to European Russia, moreover, was calculated to be only four to six minutes. In a crisis, the Soviets could be attacked with little or no warning

and therefore would have to consider striking the Pershing sites before the US missiles were launched.

Other US actions also added to the tension. On 23 March 1983, President Reagan announced the Strategic Defense Initiative, a program to develop a ground- and space-based, laser-armed, anti-ballistic missile shield that the media quickly dubbed "Star Wars." Andropov, now General Secretary, lashed out four days later. He accused the United States of preparing a first strike on the USSR and asserted that Reagan was "inventing new plans on how to unleash a nuclear war in the best way, with the hope of winning it."

The US continued psychological-warfare operations initiated in the early months of the Reagan administration. In April and May 1983, the US Pacific Fleet held its largest exercises to date in the northwest Pacific. Forty ships, including three aircraft carrier battle groups, participated, along with AWACS-equipped B-52s. At one point, the fleet sailed within 720 kilometers (450 miles) of the Kamchatka Peninsula and Petropavlovsk, the only Soviet naval base with direct access to open seas. US attack submarines and antisubmarine aircraft conducted operations in protected areas ("bastions") where the Soviet Navy had stationed a large number of its nuclear-powered ballistic missile submarines. US aircraft from the carriers *Midway* and *Enterprise* carried out a simulated bombing run over a military installation on the small Soviet-occupied island of Zelenny in the Kuril Island chain.

These types of incidents, troop buildups, and exercises would understandably play a role in heightened tensions that could have led to World War III. Thankfully, that never happened, and it is believed that Able Archer 83 ended by the time the Soviet Union could fully ready their troops to retaliate.

NORWEGIAN ROCKET SCARE—1995

Although technically occurring after the Cold War, the 1995 Norwegian rocket scare absolutely deserves a mention in this chapter. It occurred on January 25, 1995, when a team of Norwegian and US scientists launched a four-stage rocket known as a Black Brant XII. It blasted off from the northwest coast of Norway, and its purpose was to carry scientific equipment to study the aurora borealis.

Figure 6.4.   An example of a Black Brant XII launching from Wal-
lops Flight Facility. *Credit*: NASA

When launches like this occur, the origin country (in this case Norway)
would send out a notice to all surrounding countries to ensure that no mis-
understandings took place. In this particular case, thirty countries, including Russia, were notified of the launch and the scientific intention behind it.
However, in Russia, no one informed the radar crews monitoring the skies
for incoming intercontinental ballistic missiles that they would see a scientific mission unfold on their screens.

As a result, once the rocket was launched, it was detected by the Olene-
gorsk early-warning radar station in Murmansk Oblast, Russia. To the op-
erators, the Norwegian-launched scientific research rocket appeared to have
the same speed and trajectory as a US Navy submarine-launched nuclear

Trident missile. As a result, the former Soviet Union, with tensions still running hot despite the end of the Cold War, went on high alert.

Russia's "nuclear briefcase," known as the Cheget, was given to Russian President Boris Yeltsin. This briefcase connects the Russian president to the special communications system code-named Kavkaz, which allows for direct communication between senior Russian officials while they make the decision to use nuclear weapons. As of the writing of this book, this is the only known incident that required Russia to activate their "nuclear briefcase."

In a series of articles created by the US European Command, or EUCOM, known as the "Week in EUCOM History," the January 23–29, 1995, edition outlined just how close the world came to seeing a Russian nuclear launch:

The Norwegian rocket incident (or Black Brant scare) refers to a few minutes of post–Cold War nuclear tension that took place on January 25, 1995, more than four years after the end of the Cold War. The incident started when a team of Norwegian and American scientists launched a Black Brant XII four-stage sounding rocket from the Andøya Rocket Range off the northwest coast of Norway. The rocket, which carried equipment to study the aurora borealis over Svalbard, flew on a high northbound trajectory, which included an air corridor that stretches from the North Dakota Minuteman-III silos all the way to Moscow, eventually reaching an altitude of 1,453 kilometers (903 mi). Nuclear forces in Russia were put on alert, and the nuclear-command suitcase was brought to President Boris Yeltsin, who then had to decide whether to launch a nuclear barrage against the United States. Notably, there is still no clear and direct confirmation that the trajectory of the rocket was taken by mistake, caused by computer or other technical failure.

This event resulted in a full alert being passed up through the military chain of command all the way to President Boris Yeltsin, who was notified immediately and the "nuclear briefcase" used to authorize nuclear launch was automatically activated. It is reported that President Boris Yeltsin activated his "nuclear keys" for the first time in his tenure. No warning was issued to the Russian populace of any incident; it was reported in the news a week afterward.

As a result of the alert, Russian submarine commanders were ordered to go into a state of combat readiness and prepare for nuclear retaliation.

Russian doctrine reportedly allowed Yeltsin ten minutes from the time of detection to decide on a course of action. Russian observers were quickly able to determine that the rocket was heading away from Russian airspace and was not a threat. Reports differ greatly as to whether or not Yeltsin came close to authorizing an attack, but the general consensus is that Yeltsin was able to conclude that there was no basis for attack, and therefore no danger.

These incidents show just how close the world was to nuclear war, yet they never knew it. The question often arises, should a nuclear attack be inevitable, would the American government inform their people, since the aftermath would undoubtedly be a national security risk? It is quite possible that the above incidents that were entirely unknown to the public when they were unfolding may answer the question on whether or not humanity would be informed of their doom.

7

THE COLD WAR
UNDER THE SEA

As students and curious minds study the history books about the Cold War, they will often see focal points on politicians, nuclear tests, arsenals, and emotionally charged speeches. However, as the leaders of both superpowers were duking it out on land, deep within the sea, there was an entirely different "war" being fought.

Lurking in the oceans, submarines became a crucial part in delivering the most powerful weapons in the world, should nuclear war break out. This critical role they played for national defense is also why submarines found themselves as part of America's "nuclear triad," the three-pronged military force that allowed the United States full capability to launch a nuclear strike whether it be by sea-, air-, or land-based systems.

Submarine commanders from both fronts were single-handedly controlling weaponry of catastrophic proportions. Land and air nuclear delivery systems could be entirely wiped out, and yet, submarines could still deliver enough firepower to destroy the planet many times over. For example, the Soviet "Akula," or Typhoon-class submarine deployed primarily in the 1980s, had the capability of harnessing twenty R-39 or SS-N-20 ballistic missiles, each with the capability of carrying ten nuclear warheads. Yes, calculated out, that meant that a single Typhoon-class Soviet submarine had two hundred nuclear warheads at their disposal. Those two hundred nuclear warheads, once launched, could be individually targeted to ten specific locations.

Frighteningly, the Americans had a near identical underwater war chest with the American Ohio-class submarine. This underwater behemoth could carry within it twenty-four UGM-96, Trident I submarine launched ballistic missiles (SLMBs), each containing eight warheads, also with individual targeting capability. That means that through much of the Cold War, a single Ohio-class submarine could fully launch their payload and, as a result, unleash complete destruction on 192 individual targets.

If that was not deadly enough, toward the end of the Cold War, the United States replaced the Trident I and deployed the UGM-133 or Trident II SLMBs. These could contain up to twelve nuclear warheads each, which would total 288 nuclear warheads that could be launched. The destructive power wielded by a single submarine, on both sides of the Cold War, was unfathomable.

Figure 7.1. Louisiana test-fires a Trident II D5 submarine launched ballistic missile. (Undated US Navy photograph, Louisiana [SSBN-743] website.) *Credit*: US Navy

Trident II SLBMs are considered one of the deadliest aspects to America's nuclear arsenal. Their lineage goes back to 1956, when America first deployed their SLBM programs. In the 2016 edition of the *Nuclear Matters Handbook*, an "overview of the US nuclear enterprise and how the United States' safe, secure, and effective nuclear deterrent is maintained," is published by the Office of the Deputy Assistant Secretary of Defense for Nuclear Matters (ODASD[NM]). Within this book, it states the following about the origin and the longevity of the SLBM programs:

> Submarine-launched ballistic missiles have been an integral part of the strategic deterrent for six generations, starting in 1956 with the US Navy Fleet Ballistic Missile (FBM) Polaris (A1) program. Since then, the SLBM has evolved through Polaris (A2), Polaris (A3), Poseidon (C3), Trident I (C4), and today's force of Trident II (D5). Each generation has been continuously deployed as a survivable force and has been routinely operationally tested and evaluated to maintain confidence and credibility in the deterrent.
>
> Today's Trident II missiles are launched from Ohio-class submarines, each carrying 24 missiles. The Trident II is a three-stage, solid-propellant, inertially guided ballistic missile with a range of more than 4,000 nautical miles, or 4,600 statute miles. Trident II is launched by the pressure of expanding gas within the launch tube. When the missile attains sufficient distance from the submarine, the first stage motor ignites, the aerospike extends, and the boost stage begins. Within about two minutes, after the third stage motor kicks in, the missile is traveling in excess of 20,000 feet (6,096 meters) per second.
>
> Trident II was first deployed in 1990 and is planned to be deployed past 2020.

Wielding such power often would play a role in how certain submarine commanders would operate within the oceans deep. Commanders on both sides would often find themselves in their own battle with each other; fought far away from the White House, the Kremlin, or the world stage. On many occasions, Soviet and American submarines would be literally on top of each other, observing movements and eavesdropping on each other's communications. To the US Navy, this surveillance during the height of the Cold War was code-named "Holystone," and with tensions running hot, it became incredibly dangerous.

In a naval postgraduate school thesis, written by Diana Beth Wueger in March of 2015, the Holystone program, including the dangers of it, were outlined:

> under the Holystone program, American intelligence-gathering missions using attack submarines had resulted in a string of collisions with Soviet subs. The Holystone missions, begun under Eisenhower, reportedly gave submarine captains the authority to use their weapons, including nuclear weapons, if threatened; these weapons did not require a second authentication in order to launch. While doctrinally the Navy insisted that commanders would receive positive launch authorization from the National Command Authority before any SLBMs could be launched, there were no technical or physical limitations beyond the coordination of personnel across the submarine itself. Personnel discipline was expected to constrain commanders from unauthorized launch.

With American submarine commanders given the ability to launch their nuclear weapons, without presidential authorization, it made for a potentially deadly situation. As tensions mounted throughout the years of the Cold War, neither side would want to appear weak or incapable, so often they would flex their muscles while on patrol. As a result, games were often played by one side to taunt the other. This would cause close calls, near misses, and sometimes, even collisions under the water. These events would bring the world inches away from World War III, and yet, most of humanity had no idea of how close they came to complete nuclear annihilation.

THE USS JAMES MADISON

In November of 1974, the USS James Madison was on mission off the coast of Scotland. It docked at Holy Loch, and once the submarine departed to head back out to sea, disaster struck. Somehow, the USS James Madison collided with a Soviet submarine waiting just offshore.

There is a lot of secrecy and controversy behind the sequence of events that unfolded. Although the Washington Post had originally reported the incident, not many details were known, and the incident remained largely covered up for decades. However, a declassified memorandum within the holdings of the Central Intelligence Agency (CIA), which is one of the only documents released about it, briefly outlines the incident. National Security Advisor Brent Scowcroft wrote the following to Secretary of State Henry Kissinger:

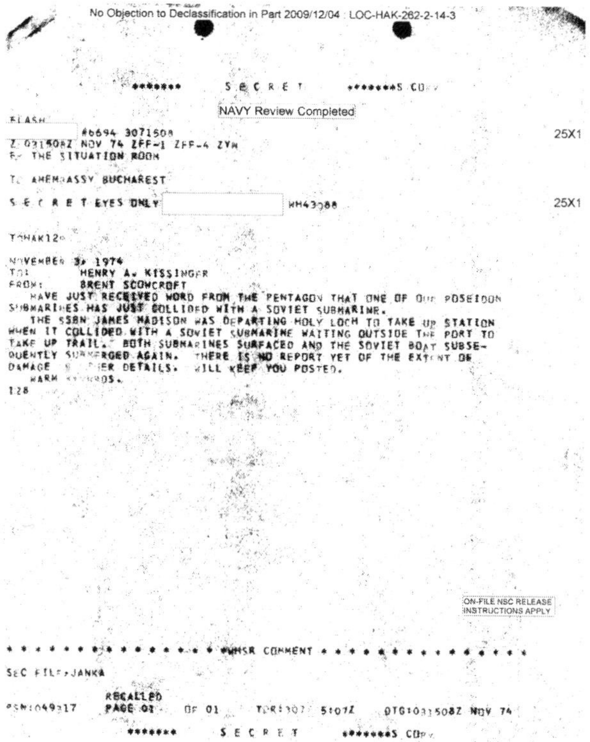

No Objection to Declassification in Part 2009/12/04 : LOC-HAK-262-2-14-3

******* SECRET *******S COPY

NAVY Review Completed

FLASH

#6694 3071508 25X1

Z 031508Z NOV 74 ZFF-1 ZFF-4 ZYH

FM THE SITUATION ROOM

TO AMEMBASSY BUCHAREST

S E C R E T EYES ONLY WH43088 25X1

TOHAK120

NOVEMBER 3, 1974

TO: HENRY A. KISSINGER

FROM: BRENT SCOWCROFT

HAVE JUST RECEIVED WORD FROM THE PENTAGON THAT ONE OF OUR POSEIDON SUBMARINES HAS JUST COLLIDED WITH A SOVIET SUBMARINE.

THE SSBN JAMES MADISON WAS DEPARTING HOLY LOCH TO TAKE UP STATION WHEN IT COLLIDED WITH A SOVIET SUBMARINE WAITING OUTSIDE THE PORT TO TAKE UP TRAIL. BOTH SUBMARINES SURFACED AND THE SOVIET BOAT SUBSEQUENTLY SUBMERGED AGAIN. THERE IS NO REPORT YET OF THE EXTENT OF DAMAGE OR OTHER DETAILS. WILL KEEP YOU POSTED.

WARM REGARDS.

128

ON-FILE NSC RELEASE INSTRUCTIONS APPLY

* * * * * * * * * * * * * * WHSR COMMENT * * * * * * * * * * * * * * *

SEC FILE, JANKA

RECALLED

PSN:049317 PAGE 01 OF 01 TOR:307/15:07Z DTG:031508Z NOV 74

******* S E C R E T *******S COPY

Figure 7.2. A declassified memorandum from the CIA outlines the incident involving the USS *James Madison*. *Credit*: Central Intelligence Agency (CIA)

Have just received word from the Pentagon that one of our Poseidon submarines has just collided with a Soviet submarine. The SSBN *James Madison* was departing Holy Loch to take up station when it collided with a Soviet submarine waiting outside the port to take up trail. Both submarines surfaced and the Soviet boat subsequently submerged again. There is no report yet of the extent of damage. Will keep you posted.

Warm regards.

There was not much released at the time about the event, and even decades later, still not much is known. However, rumors persisted that this incident was involved in a massive cover-up, spearheaded by Kissinger himself.

To support that, the CIA watched the media headlines and archived pertinent material. Within CIA holdings, there is a clipped *Newsweek* article from 1975 that refers to this effort to conceal the facts:

Did Kissinger Deep-Six the News?

Twice during the past year, Henry Kissinger squelched Pentagon plans to release information involving American and Russian submarines for fear the stories would damage US-Soviet relations, according to Defense Department sources. The Pentagon insists Kissinger blocked release of facts about the CIA effort to raise the sunken Russian sub in the Pacific and news about a 1974 collision between the US submarine *James Madison* and a Russian sub in the North Sea. Defense officials were ready to take a bow for the recovery of the Russian sub; most accidents at sea are routinely made public.

Although some events were "routinely made public," it would take many years before the media and the world would hear the full story about many of these underwater near misses, like with the USS *James Madison*. It was clear that such events could have had monumental consequences, which included paving the way to the inadvertent start of nuclear war.

Any collision, near miss, or incident could be construed as an act of aggression by the other side. Submarine commanders could transmit a message back to their respective upper brass stateside to indicate that they were possibly under attack. With tensions running so hot throughout much of the Cold War, these types of messages received could have quickly escalated to launch orders within minutes. Therefore, as a result, whatever could be kept secret, was.

THE K-219

The Soviet K-219 was a Navaga-class ballistic missile submarine. It measured 425 feet in length and was officially commissioned on December 31,

1971. The K-219 would patrol the waters, carrying with it sixteen SS-N-6 SLBMs, containing a combined thirty-four nuclear warheads.

Fifteen years after it was first commissioned, the K-219 found itself entangled in one of the more controversial incidents during the Cold War. On October 3, 1986, while on a routine patrol in the North Atlantic, disaster struck. The K-219 was about 680 miles northeast of Bermuda when an explosion ripped through missile tube number six. This caused it immediately to take on water; a disastrous scenario for any submerged submarine.

In a 2005 article written and published by the US Navy in *Undersea Warfare* magazine, Russian Navy Captain 1st Rank (Ret.) Igor Kurdin and US Navy Lt. Cmdr. Wayne Grasdock jointly wrote an article entitled, "Loss of a Yankee SSBN." Within it, they gave rare details on the incident with the K-219:

> After 30 days at sea, K-219 moved into its designated patrol area in the Sargasso Sea in the North Atlantic. At 0456, on Oct. 3, the submarine came to periscope depth for routine communications. Five minutes later, it began a descent to 85 meters. At the time, the GEhU (electric plant) was operating in one-echelon mode, and the capacity of the starboard reactor was at 30 percent; the port reactor had been suppressed/damped by all the absorbers, and the steam production plant (PPU) and the turbine were ready for operation; the starboard turbine operated the screw, and the port shaft line was ready to operate the propulsion motor.
>
> At 0514, the BCh-2 officer and the hold machinist/engineer in compartment IV (the forward missile compartment) discovered water dripping from under the plug of missile tube No. 6 (the third tube from the bow on the port side). During precompression of the plug, the drips turned into a stream. The BCh-2 officer reported water in missile tube No. 6, and at 0525, the Captain ordered an ascent to a safe depth (46 meters) while a pump was started in an attempt to dry out missile tube No. 6. At 0532, brown clouds of oxidant began issuing from under the missile-tube plug, and the BCh-2 officer declared an accident alert in the compartment and reported the situation to the GKP (main control station). Although personnel assigned to other compartments left the space, nine people remained in compartment IV. The Captain declared an accident alert. It took the crew no more than one minute to carry out initial damage control measures, which included hermetically sealing all compartments. Five minutes later, at 0538, an explosion occurred in missile tube No. 6.

The article goes on to give details on how the submarine was severely crippled, and how the crew attempted to save it. However, on October 5, two long days after the initial explosion, the K-219 had its final moments above sea level. The article goes on to state:

> At dawn on Oct. 5, the damage control party continued to prepare the submarine for towing. At 1815, the motor vessel *Krasnovardeysk* began towing the crippled submarine. However, the submarine's draft and bow trim slowly continued to increase, and the next morning at 0620, the towing cable snapped, and the bow and stern hatches were submerged. The damage-control party was not able to descend to compartment III because the lower conning tower hatch was jammed. The submarine continued to lose buoyancy. When it was submerged to the level of the superstructure deck, the damage control party left. By 1100, the submarine had submerged to the level of the fairwater planes, and the GK (commander in chief) of the VMF ordered the Captain to abandon ship. At 1102 on Oct. 6, 1986 the K-219 sank.

A total of four seamen were lost in the explosion and the aftermath. Given the circumstances, and the fact that the ship held 120 officers and men, that was a somewhat positive outcome. Yet, the biggest catastrophe from this event was not the loss of lives, or the loss of sixteen SLBMs that were now at the bottom of the sea: it was the accusation made by the Soviet Union against the United States.

Although no official announcement was made, various media outlets, including CBS News, began reporting that the Soviet K-219 collided with the American USS *Augusta*. The source of the accusation was never revealed, but the story, and the allegation of a collision, made its way into a book called *Hostile Waters* released in 1997 and then into an HBO movie released that same year. Although based on truth, the book and movie were considered "Hollywoodized" and not entirely accurate.

In the *Undersea Warfare* article referenced above, the authors referred to the embellished and erroneous facts within the story:

> Although the book *Hostile Waters*, published in 1997, is based on the true story of K-219, this article is a more accurate technical representation of what took place—it leaves out the "Hollywood" aspects and describes the heroic efforts of a crew attempting to save a submarine. Despite the attempts of the

officers and crew to gain more recognition, only one sailor, who died in the reactor compartment, received an award. This decoration and the facts of the incident are not spoken of in Russia. Captain Britanov states that in the eyes of his government, there were no heroes on K-219. When asked the number of times he is called to be a guest lecturer at Russian functions, he simply states, "None—I do not tell the story the way my government wants me to tell it. I did not collide with an American sub."

Despite the captain of the boat denying the collision, the controversy lingered. In fact, the release of the book and movie forced the US Navy to release a short statement addressing the issue, which by their own admission, was somewhat unprecedented. In a press release sent out by the navy:

The US Navy has issued the following statement regarding the release of the book "Hostile Waters" and an HBO movie of the same name, based on the incidents surrounding the casualty of the Russian Yankee submarine (K-219) off the Bahamas in October 1986:

"The United States Navy normally does not comment on submarine operations, but in the case, because the scenario is so outrageous, the Navy is compelled to respond.

The United States Navy categorically denies that any US submarine collided with the Russian Yankee submarine (K-219) or that the Navy had anything to do with the cause of the casualty that resulted in the loss of the Russian Yankee submarine."

Although the mystery may never be solved, one document released by the US Navy outlining the history of the USS *Augusta* produces more questions than answers. The record is known as a "Command History," and it outlines the major events throughout the year it is written for the USS *Augusta*.

"Command History" documents are incredibly useful to researchers, as they contain an enormous amount of history within. Many submarines, ships, commands, military bases, and such publish internally (which can be obtained via the Freedom of Information Act [FOIA]) these Command Histories. In the case of the USS *Augusta*, I tracked down the "Command History" for 1986. It first begins with an overview of the USS *Augusta*:

USS AUGUSTA (SSN 7101), the thirtieth 688 Class fast attack submarine, is one of the most advanced undersea vessels of its type in the world. Her

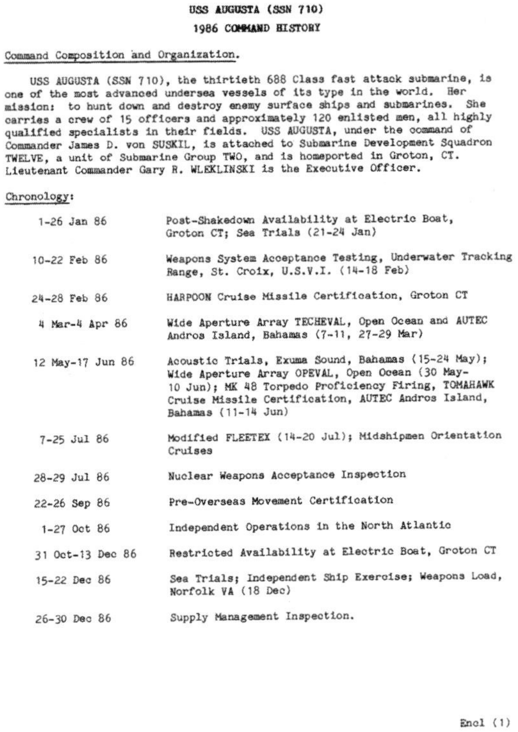

USS AUGUSTA (SSN 710)
1986 COMMAND HISTORY

Command Composition and Organization.

   USS AUGUSTA (SSN 710), the thirtieth 688 Class fast attack submarine, is
one of the most advanced undersea vessels of its type in the world. Her
mission: to hunt down and destroy enemy surface ships and submarines. She
carries a crew of 15 officers and approximately 120 enlisted men, all highly
qualified specialists in their fields. USS AUGUSTA, under the command of
Commander James D. von SUSKIL, is attached to Submarine Development Squadron
TWELVE, a unit of Submarine Group TWO, and is homeported in Groton, CT.
Lieutenant Commander Gary R. WLEKLINSKI is the Executive Officer.

Chronology:

1-26 Jan 86	Post-Shakedown Availability at Electric Boat, Groton CT; Sea Trials (21-24 Jan)
10-22 Feb 86	Weapons System Acceptance Testing, Underwater Tracking Range, St. Croix, U.S.V.I. (14-18 Feb)
24-28 Feb 86	HARPOON Cruise Missile Certification, Groton CT
4 Mar-4 Apr 86	Wide Aperture Array TECHEVAL, Open Ocean and AUTEC Andros Island, Bahamas (7-11, 27-29 Mar)
12 May-17 Jun 86	Acoustic Trials, Exuma Sound, Bahamas (15-24 May); Wide Aperture Array OPEVAL, Open Ocean (30 May-10 Jun); MK 48 Torpedo Proficiency Firing, TOMAHAWK Cruise Missile Certification, AUTEC Andros Island, Bahamas (11-14 Jun)
7-25 Jul 86	Modified FLEETEX (14-20 Jul); Midshipmen Orientation Cruises
28-29 Jul 86	Nuclear Weapons Acceptance Inspection
22-26 Sep 86	Pre-Overseas Movement Certification
1-27 Oct 86	Independent Operations in the North Atlantic
31 Oct-13 Dec 86	Restricted Availability at Electric Boat, Groton CT
15-22 Dec 86	Sea Trials; Independent Ship Exercise; Weapons Load, Norfolk VA (18 Dec)
26-30 Dec 86	Supply Management Inspection.

Encl (1)

Figure 7.3. A page from the "Command History"
of the USS *Augusta* (SSN 710).

mission: to hunt down and destroy enemy surface ships and submarines. She
carries a crew of 15 officers and approximately 120 enlisted men, all highly
qualified specialists in their fields. USS AUGUSTA, under the command of
Commander James D. von SUSKIL, is attached to Submarine Development
Squadron TWELVE, a unit of Submarine Group TWO, and is homeported
in Groton, CT. Lieutenant Commander Gary R. WLEKLINSKI is the Executive Officer.

The document then offered a chronological breakdown of the year 1986.
This includes dates for weapons system testing, orientation cruises, inspec-
tions, certifications, and more. Throughout almost the entire month of
October, the chronology also puts the USS *Augusta* in the area of the Soviet
K-219:

1–27 Oct 86 Independent Operations in the North Atlantic

Then, toward the end of the "Command History" document, an interesting fact comes up around the time the alleged collision took place.

October marked USS AUGUSTA'S first operational commitment. She was tasked to conduct an emergent independent submarine operation which lasted through the end of the month.

USS AUGUSTA was awarded the 1986 Supply BLUE E for Excellence in supply support and food service. This accolade was shortly followed by a Supply Management Inspection in which she earned grades of Outstanding and Excellent across the board.

The year concluded with USS AUGUSTA'S return to Electric Boat Shipyard for repairs and installation of a new sonar dome. By Christmas she had begun preparations for the ship's second Operational Reactor Safeguards Examination and another round of certifications prior to deployment as an operational unit assigned to CINCLANTFLT.

Some have theorized that the "repairs" required around the time frame of the alleged collision may lend credence to the allegation. Although no accident, collision, or mishap of any kind is referenced in the "Command History" (and likely, it generally would be should one have occurred), it is possible it was omitted due to the sensitivity of it.

COLD WAR ENDS—PROBLEMS CONTINUE

Many of the incidents involving nuclear-equipped submarines were due to high tensions during the Cold War. However, once the Cold War was over, there was no slowdown in incidents that occurred. Some cases happened without casualty, while others ended in tragedy.

In April of 2019, the Naval Submarine Medical Research Laboratory authored, "A Critical Review of Casualties from Non-Combat Submarine Incidents and Current US Navy Medical Response Capability with Specific Focus on the Application of Prolonged Field Care to Disabled Submarine Survival and Rescue." Although a mouthful of a title, the authors, which include British Royal Navy Surgeon Commander Lesley A. Whybourn; David

M. Fothergill, Ph.D.; US Navy Commander Anthony J. Quatroche (ret.); and US Navy Lieutenant Nathan A. Moss, outlined many incidents from before, during, and after the Cold War that involved nuclear submarines. And despite the end of the Cold War, along with the easing tensions within the deep, incidents continued to occur:

> Entrapment of part or all of a submarine crew in a disabled submarine (DIS-SUB) is an established risk of submarine operations in peace and war. Few USN sinkings have occurred since World War II and none since the loss of USS *Scorpion* (SSN 589) in 1968, testament to the safety of modern submarine designs and operations. The intervening years have however seen further international losses, most notably the BAP *Pacocha* in 1988 and the K-141 *Kursk* in 2000. At the time of writing, an international search and rescue operation had recently been mounted for the missing ARA *San Juan*. USN and international submarine force involvement in major incidents of fire, flooding, collision and grounding and loss of propulsion also continues at an average rate of 1.7 a year, of which over half are considered to have significantly risked the loss of a submarine. Analysis of USN mishaps by NSMRL in 2007 showed the rate of mishaps with DISSUB potential to have remained relatively constant since the Cold War. The ongoing risk and extremely high cost of a future event, together with commitment to international response efforts, makes Submarine Escape and Rescue (SER) capability a core safety requirement for submarine operating nations.

THE K-141 *KURSK*

One of the more recent and most deadly events that occurred post–Cold War was the sinking of the K-141 *Kursk* on August 12, 2000. About nine years after the Cold War had "ended," the K-141 had a tragedy that ultimately resulted in the loss of the entire crew—all 118 on board. As with most incidents such as these, there are varying versions of what really happened.

The K-141 was an Oscar II-class, nuclear-powered submarine. It was the second largest submarine in the Soviet navy when launched in 1994, second only to the Typhoon-class. It measured just more than five hundred feet in length and had on board twenty-four SS-N-19 cruise missiles, each with the capability of being fitted with a thermonuclear warhead.

Although Russia never officially acknowledged that nuclear warheads were on board, the K-141 was nuclear powered, which translates to the fact it had two on-board nuclear reactors. That meant any type of explosion on board could have disastrous consequences.

On August 10, 2000, the K-141 joined what was called the "Summer-X" exercise. This involved numerous Russian warships and submarines, along with troops from the Federal Border Guard Service, RF police, and other air defense units from Belarus. During this exercise, the Russian navy was demonstrating its skills on the water, which included anti-submarine warfare, torpedo strikes, and amphibious landings. Partly propaganda and partly a true exercise, the K-141 played a role in the demonstrations.

On their first day into the exercise, the *Kursk* launched a Granit missile that had a dummy warhead, an obvious show of might. Two days after that, on August 12, they were preparing to launch dummy torpedoes that had no explosive warheads, but rather, was just another show of strength. While preparing to launch, an explosion severely crippled the submarine.

It was later concluded that the cause of this was a failure of one of the Type 65 torpedoes, fueled by hydrogen peroxide. There was a leak, which caused a form of highly concentrated hydrogen peroxide known as "high-test peroxide" or HTP, to seep out until it met a catalyst of some type. This caused the HTP to expand rapidly by a factor of 5,000, causing massive amounts of steam and oxygen, which then ruptured a kerosene fuel tank.

The deadly concoction that resulted caused a massive explosion that was equivalent to about two hundred and fifty to five hundred pounds of TNT. Approximately two minutes later, a second explosion occurred, which measured approximately three to seven tons of TNT. This resulted in the death, almost instantly, of each sailor within the first three compartments of the ship. This left only twenty-three sailors that remained alive on board.

Rescue attempts were carried out by Russia to save the remaining crew. Offers to help were made by France, Germany, Italy, Israel, Norway, and the United States. However, Russia refused it. Whether it be pride, ego, or something else, valuable time was lost. It was reported that there were signs that some of the crew were still alive, even days after the explosions, as some reported hearing "tapping" from within the submarine's hull spelling out, "SOS . . . water." This is also supported by documents released by the US Navy (see later in this chapter), however, this claim is highly disputed, since the K-141 had a double hull. This fact leads some to believe that the likelihood of hearing the tapping was nil.

Regardless of if tapping was heard, bad weather hindered continued Russian rescue efforts. It was not until five days after the initial accident amid mounting pressure from major media, that Russia finally gave in and accepted help from Great Britain and Norway. However, it would take another two days for British and Norwegian ships to arrive, since Russia delayed so long in accepting the offer.

Despite efforts by Norwegian and British divers once they arrived, hope was eventually lost. On August 21, Norwegian divers finally confirmed that there was no one left alive on board. The K-141 *Kursk*, along with the entire crew, was lost.

On the surface, what happened to the K-141 appeared to be an accident, possibly due to a lack of funding and proper upkeep of Russian naval vessels and their weaponry. However, some Russian officials began floating another idea that played well into documented history: a collision.

It took only two days for that rumor to be floated, which first came from Russian Fleet Admiral Vladimir Kuroyedov. He claimed that the *Kursk* was brought down by a NATO submarine; a claim he continued to make for years after the event.

Defense Minister Igor Sergeyev also backed up the theory, stating, "An increasing amount of evidence suggests that the submarine must have collided with an external object." The collision theory never became an official stance of Russia, but there were high-ranking officials who were not quiet about the belief.

The collision theory was dismissed by the United States. Secretary of Defense William S. Cohen responded to the allegation on September 22, 2000, while at a press conference in Tokyo, Japan:

> With respect to the *Kursk*, we had made it very clear that the United States, that our ships had no role in that terrible tragedy. We have communicated that, we believe that our word, indeed, has been categorical. I have received every assurance and I know that all our ships are operational and could not possibly have been involved in any kind of contact with the Russian submarine. So frankly, there is no need for inspections, since ours are completely operational, there was no contact whatsoever with the *Kursk*. I hope that the Russian authorities find out the cause of it.

All I can do is speculate at this point, that there were internal blasts that led to the loss of that ship and the fine men aboard her.

With no inspection of American ships, and the official denial of involvement, much of the international press dismissed the collision theory. Russian pride and ego were largely to blame for Russia not taking responsibility. However, not everyone is willing to dismiss American or NATO involvement.

FOIA requests reveal an enormous amount of secrecy surrounding the events with the sinking of the K-141 *Kursk*. The National Security Agency (NSA) fully denied releasing the records relating to the incident back in 2014. Another attempt was made in 2018, and a final denial by the NSA was issued in April of 2019 stating that all NSA documents, which totaled an unknown number of pages, were being withheld as they were classified "Top Secret" and "Secret." Not a single word was releasable about a very public event. Although secrets such as submarine locations, capabilities, and such should be withheld, it is unlikely that every page within NSA holdings would not be releasable.

Other agencies were not quite so dismissive of efforts to pry loose documents. The Department of the Navy released fifteen pages to The Black Vault, all consisting of "Maritime Intelligence Reports" from the days after the initial explosions on board the *Kursk*. The US Navy issued multiple reports on August 14, the earliest of their records, and days that followed, updating new pieces of information coming in regarding the tragedy. One of the reports offers a clue as to how classified details remain within American files:

> During the mid 0700 ZULU hours of 12 August, OSCAR II [REDACTED] KURSK Impacted the sea floor in the Barents Sea, apparently unable to resurface. The submarine was participating in the Russian Navy's SUMMEREX 2000. The Russian General Staff has been quoted as saying that a crew of 166 was on board.
>
> During mid 0700 ZULU hour of 12 August, at least two distinct acoustic events were detected in what is now known to be the casualty area.

What then followed were multiple paragraphs entirely classified and redacted. It is always a bad practice for an investigator to assume what may be under redactions, at least, that is a practice I try to stay away from. More often than not, when documents that were previously blacked out are further released and revealed, many times I wonder why the information was redacted in the first place. So, I never want to speculate, but sometimes you can't help it.

Figure 7.4. The cover of a declassified "Maritime Intelligence Report" dated August 14, 2000, which outlines the incident involving the K-141 *Kursk*. *Credit*: US Navy

One must question whether the redacted information may point to another American or NATO vessel in the location of the *Kursk* that may have played a role in the K-141's sinking. Paragraph markings indicate that the information redacted is considered "Top Secret" and "Secret," so whatever is withheld is highly classified.

The CIA also released documents to The Black Vault, but another strange piece of evidence was revealed. In their response, the CIA released fifteen pages of material relating to the *Kursk* sinking. However, according to the CIA response letter, these fifteen pages comprised two documents. One from December 7, 2000, and another two-page translated from a Russian newspaper article, as archived by the CIA. This was from a Russian media outlet and contained no CIA commentary, notes, or additions, and consisted solely of the translated text.

According to the CIA, there were no CIA-generated pages that existed prior to December 7, 2000, which should have included real-time CIA-gathered intelligence on the K-141 disaster. As indicated by the US Navy documents released, near real-time intelligence was being gathered, so this is rather strange for the CIA to not be doing the same. The CIA's primary mission is to gather foreign intelligence, so this should have been a priority with such a major occurrence. It is heavily documented and historically proven that the CIA has records on many world events, and will often have real-time intelligence gathering. Yet, not a single page existed around the time of sinking.

Despite this abnormality, the record that was released was an "Intelligence Report" from the Office of Russian and European Analysis, Office of Transnational Issues. It also dealt with the collision theory, though largely dismissed it. The document states:

> An internal weapons malfunction is most likely to have been the trigger for the sinking of the Russian Oscar-11 nuclear submarine *Kursk* in the Barents Sea on 12 August.
>
> Russian officials almost certainly do not yet know what sank the *Kursk*. Continued claims that the triggering event was a collision with a US or British submarine probably result from a combination of genuine suspicion, bureaucratic blame shifting, and the lack of irrefutable disconfirming evidence. Consequently, these views will be hard to dislodge.
>
> - We assess that the Russians have enough seismic and acoustic data to conclude that the *Kursk* was lost due to two explosions, but they lack the quantity and quality of data to point to a triggering event or to rule out the presence of another submarine in the vicinity of the *Kursk*. Consequently, they are unable to completely rule out a collision as the initiating event.
> - The commission charged with determining the cause of the accident headed by Deputy Premier Klebanov—stopped short at its meeting on 8 November of claiming a collision with a US or British submarine, but the theory that the *Kursk* collided with an "underwater object" nonetheless remains "first among equals" with the Russians.
> - In a press conference after the meeting, Klebanov said the collision theory "received very serious confirmation" from expert testimony and video showing

a "very serious dent" and scrapes in the rubber hull coating. We assess that the damage probably is the result of the second explosion or bottom impact.

Figure 7.5. Pages released from the CIA show that information regarding the sinking of the K-141 _Kursk_ is still highly classified. _Credit_: Central Intelligence Agency (CIA)

The CIA document obviously offers the tone of dismissing the collision theory, but then it details Russian claims. Despite the claim that there was no American or NATO involvement, there is a high percentage of information that is still classified within this CIA file. It is possible additional evidence does exist that supports the collision theory, but the CIA wants to ensure the world never sees it.

The report then goes on to outline some of the evidence that Russia was releasing that supported the collision theory:

Against a backdrop of strong distrust of the West in Russia and a history of similar collisions—most recently in 1992 and 1993—and given the collision theory's attractiveness for personal and professional reasons in shifting the blame, Russian military and civilian leaders are likely to resist abandoning the theory.

In this context, Russian officials—spearheaded now by the navy—have put together a body of circumstantial "evidence" to support the contention that a collision occurred.

- The video to which Klebanov and others have referred—first aired publicly on 25 October—appears to show concave damage and discoloration that superficially supports their claim. Russian naval officers watching described the apparent dent as "the point of contact and the scrape marks as they [submarines] rubbed against each other." We assess that the damage probably is the result of the second explosion or bottom impact.
- According to Russian media in early December: the Navy has cut out a hull segment containing the alleged dent, as well as one of the torpedo tubes, and brought them to the surface for further analysis.
- Russian officials also point to what they say was a sonar contact with a foreign submarine near *Kursk* after the explosion and a US submarine's stop in a Norwegian port, which they suspect could have been for emergency repairs. They also cite the US refusal of Moscow's official request to view the two US submarines identified in the press as monitoring the Russian naval exercises in the Barents at the time of the *Kursk* disaster.

This last paragraph cited plays into why Secretary of Defense Cohen responded the way he did at his press conference, denying any inspection or visual reveal of the submarines that were in the area of the *Kursk* when it went down.

If there was no involvement, it does beg us all to ask the question, "Why?" Even if it is just to squash any rumors or conspiracies being touted by Russian officials, it was strange that America would not want to put the issue to rest.

The *Kursk* disaster is hopefully the last chapter in a long history of undersea mishaps, close calls, and collisions. However, probably not. As government records outline, despite the end of the Cold War and easing tensions between world superpowers, history often repeats itself.

THE SECRET
SPACE PROGRAM

8

MILITARY MOON
COLONIZATION

The period known as the "space race" between the Soviet Union and the United States was full of triumphs and setbacks. Both nations raced to successfully launch a satellite into orbit, put the first human into space, orbit the first astronaut around the Earth, and ultimately be the first to land on the moon.

We know that in the end, America beat the world to the lunar surface with *Apollo XI* by putting astronauts Neil Armstrong and Edwin "Buzz" Aldrin on the moon, while Michael Collins orbited above. However, the Soviet Union beat America in many other facets of the "space race." On October 4, 1957, Russia successfully launched the first satellite, *Sputnik*, into orbit. On *Sputnik II*, the first animal, a dog named Laika, boldly went where no canine went before on November 13, 1957. Soviet astronaut Yuri Gagarin became the first human ever to fly in space on April 12, 1961, on board the *Vostok 1*. The Soviet Union made history on June 16, 1963, by flying the first woman into space—Valentina Tereshkova on the *Vostok 6*. Tragically, they even had the first to die in space when the *Soyuz 1* spacecraft crashed during its return to Earth on April 23, 1967. The *Salyut*, a Russian space station put into orbit in 1971, beat the American's first space station, *Skylab*, by about two years.

The list goes on with Soviet space-firsts throughout history, but both nations ultimately had triumphs that led humanity to where we are today. These strides toward putting man on the moon, and beyond, may not have been possible if it were not for the help of some of the most skilled and advanced scientists that came from Nazi Germany after the fall of the Third Reich. Both the Soviet Union and the United States had secret programs that brought over to their respective countries captured or surrendered Nazi scientists who shared their knowledge of V-2 rockets and propulsion engines. This led both nations into a race to conquer space that would last for two decades. But did these minds that previously worked for Adolf Hitler play a crucial role in influencing the strategy for space domination?

Behind the scenes and away from a scientific agenda for lunar exploration, a much more sinister plan was unfolding for the United States. The American and Soviet triumphs and "firsts" that were publicly known were only the tip of the iceberg to what was really going on. America knew that the Cold War with the Soviet Union was on, and the "space race," largely watched by the general public worldwide, was only a small aspect to winning it. Dominance of space would bring scientific and militaristic advantages that either nation would benefit from considerably.

Therefore, the United States began crafting a secret plan to build a military outpost on the surface of the moon. The plan was known as Project Horizon, and in a 1959 report by the US Army, originally classified "Secret," the "requirement" for such a base was spelled out by the military:

1. General
   There is a requirement for a manned military outpost on the moon. The lunar outpost is required to develop and protect potential United States interests on the moon; to develop techniques in moon-based surveillance of the earth and space, in communications relay, and in operations on the surface of the moon; to serve as a base for exploration of the moon, for further exploration into space and for military operations on the moon if required; and to support scientific investigations on the moon.

2. Operational Concept
   Initially the outpost will be of sufficient size and contain sufficient equipment to permit the survival and moderate constructive activity of a minimum number of personnel (about 10–20) on a sustained basis. It must be designed for expansion of facilities, resupply, and rotation of personnel to insure maximum extension of sustained occupancy. It should be designed to be self-sufficient for as long as possible without

outside support. In the location and design of the base, consideration will be given to operation of a triangulation station of a moon-to-earth base line space surveillance system, facilitation communications with and observation of the earth, facilitating travel between the moon and the earth, exploration of the moon and further explorations of space, and to the defense of the base against attack if required. The primary objective is to establish the first permanent manned installation on the moon. Incidental to this mission will be the investigation of the scientific, commercial, and military potential of the moon.

Figure 8.1.   A model diagram of the Project Horizon outpost on the lunar surface. *Credit*: US Army

This two-volume Project Horizon study was conducted by the Department of the Army. Volume 1 was entitled, "Summary and Supporting Considerations," and totaled 57 pages. Volume 2, the "Technical Considerations & Plans," was much heftier, totaling 323 pages. The plans were extremely elaborate, but overzealous.

In Volume 1 of the reports issued, the US Army stated they could have the lunar outpost operational by late 1966, with manned landing on the base even as early as Spring 1965. However, history would show that it was not until 1969 that *Apollo XI* landed on the moon for the first time with Armstrong and Aldrin, so the army was wildly off on their estimations.

In Volume 2 of the reports, it outlined considerations behind such a plan, for example, the cost.

> The total cost of establishing the twelve-man outpost and the first year of operation is slightly over $6 billion. Only in FY 1964, FY 1965, and FY 1966 is the annual requirement in excess of $1 billion. This is due primarily to the large vehicle production needed to support the firing schedule.

Six billion dollars, adjusted for 780.22 percent inflation from 1959 to 2019, would total nearly fifty-three billion dollars. Although a hefty price tag, it was not out of the ordinary for the time of the "space race" to spend lavishly. The stakes were high, so money became no object.

In a declassified Central Intelligence Agency (CIA) document, dated August 1964, a comparison was shown in a "Secret" study on the finan-

Table 2

Soviet and US Space Expenditures
as a Share of Total Defense and Space R & D Expenditures a/
by Fiscal Year
1961-64

Expenditures	Unit	1961	1962	1963	1964
USSR					
Total Defense R & D	Billion US $	4.6 to 7.0	5.3 to 8.0	6.0 to 9.1	6.5 to 10.3
Of which:					
Space	Billion US $	0.7 to 1.0	0.8 to 1.2	1.5 to 2.4	2.0 to 4.0
Space as a share of total b/	Percent	15	15	25	30 to 40
US					
Total Defense R & D	Billion US $	8.3	9.4	10.7	13.4
Of which:					
Space	Billion US $	1.5	2.4	4.1	6.2
Space as a share of total	Percent	18	26	38	46

a. For the US this total is the sum of the research, development, test, and evaluation expenditures of the Department of Defense (DOD), the Atomic Energy Commission (AEC), and the National Aeronautics and Space Administration (NASA). For the USSR this total refers in concept to classified works of national importance, primarily military, nuclear energy, and space RDT & E activities. It is derived from published Soviet financial allocations, the precise scope of which is unknown, and, therefore, the estimates contain a range to reflect this uncertainty. These allocations are expressed in current rubles and converted to dollars.
b. Although the estimates, because they contain a range, result in a corresponding range of percentages, this range is not significant for 1961-63, and, therefore, a single-valued percentage rounded to the nearest 5 has been used for these years.

Figure 8.2. A declassified table breakdown of space expenditures, comparing both Soviet and American spending. *Credit*: Central Intelligence Agency (CIA)

cial costs of the Soviet space program versus the American space program up until that year. It showed in the beginning days, the Soviet Union well outspent the Americans; however, the United States began pumping much more into the program in later years, thus potentially playing a role in beating the Russians to the lunar surface. With this fact, increasing the budget by the billions to create a lunar outpost would likely not be out of the question.

Despite the cost likely not being an issue, the technological considerations added an element that was nothing short of extraordinary. In Volume 2, the study outlined the number of launches it would take to achieve the twelve-man lunar outpost:

A lunar environment exploration program, on a scale considerably larger than is known to be currently planned, must begin by 1962. It is anticipated that the NASA will sponsor this research activity. During the period 1960 through 1964, respectively. By the end of 1964 a total of 72 SATURN vehicles should have been launched, of which 40 are expected to contribute to the accomplishment of Project HORIZON. These 40 launching will include six lunar satellites, eight lunar soft landings, seven lunar circumnavigations, four orbital return missions, and 15 operational trips for the buildup phase. The purpose of the initial 25 firings will be the development of the transportation system's techniques and procedures, as well as that of obtaining scientific and engineering environmental information. The buildup phase begins with the first orbital flight in August 1964 and the first operational cargo delivery to the moon in January 1965. Cargo will be sent to the lunar construction site directly from the earth's surface in packages of 6,000 pounds each, and via orbit in packages of 48,000 pounds each. The first manned landing is scheduled for April 1965 and will consist of a two-man vehicle with an immediate earth return capability. The buildup and construction phase will be continued without interruption until the outpost is ready for beneficial occupancy and manned by a task force of 12 men by November 1966.

This buildup program requires 61 SATURN I and 88 SATURN II launchings in a period of 28 months (August 1964 through November 1966). This requires an average launching rate of 5.3 per month. The total useful cargo transported to the moon amounts to 245 tons, assuming an average mission reliability of 80 percent.

This transportation job results in lancing material for the construction of a lunar outpost with a basic structure weight of 40 tons, and an additional 205 tons for equipment and supplies. Approximately 40 of these 205 tons will be required for life essential supplies.

A total of 64 firings have been scheduled for the first operational year of the lunar outpost, December 1966 through 1967, and results in a useful cargo transportation capability of approximately 133 additional tons from earth to the lunar surface. These vehicles also provide transportation of orbit and lunar crews to the orbit as well as rotation of the outpost personnel, with a nominal stay time of nine months on the moon. An additional six SATURN I and ten SATURN II vehicles are assigned the mission of emergency vehicles during the entire project. With the same assumed reliability, the emergency vehicles have the capability of transporting an additional 30 tons of cargo to the lunar surface.

The average transportation cost for a one-way trip to the moon for the program presented herein is $4,250 per pound. This includes the investment in the R&D program and the necessary facilities. To sustain the operation after 1968 without post expansion and based on the same carrier vehicles, this figure would be reduced to approximately $1,850 per pound. By use of nuclear or electric propulsion, a further reduction of this cost figure to $400 per pound seems feasible by 1975. Early in the program, the transportation cost for a round trip from the earth to the moon and return to earth would be approximately 48 times that of a one-way trip from earth to moon. This may be reduced to a factor of 25 by further development.

The total program cost as outlined in this report was estimated to be $6,052,300,000 over an eight-and-a-half-year period. This is an average of approximately $700 million per year. These figures are estimates based on past experience and, while preliminary, they represent the right order of magnitude. Though substantial, they should be compared with the annual sales volume of the aircraft and missile defense industry of ten billion dollars per year, or the annual defense budget of forty-two billion dollars per year.

To put that into perspective, in the history of the space program, there were only nineteen Saturn I and Saturn IB rockets flown. Although it was explored as a viable replacement to the Saturn IB, the Saturn II never lifted off once. The requirement to build the lunar outpost would have required approximately three times the launches of the Saturn I, but only in a period of just more than two years, versus the nineteen years that we saw the Saturn I and IB enter space. In addition, they would need to add an additional eighty-eight launches of the Saturn II in that two-year period; a rocket that they had never lifted off the ground.

Seeing the breakdown of the required launch schedule, the lunar base did not seem feasible even by today's standards. The cost, although an obstacle that was easily overcome, paled as a problem compared to the technological demand. Yet, that did not stop the US Army from saying that America should do it. In a letter dated March 20, 1959, signed by Lieutenant Arthur G. Trudeau, Chief of Research and Development for the US Army, as addressed to the Chief of Ordnance, US Army, it stated the following:

> I envision expeditious development of the proposal to establish a lunar outpost to be of critical importance to the US Army of the future. This evaluation is apparently shared by the Chief of Staff in view of his expeditious approval and enthusiastic endorsement of initiation of the study. Therefore, the detail to be covered by the investigation and the subsequent plan should be as complete as is feasible in the time limits allowed and within the funds currently available within the office of the Chief of Ordnance. In this time of limited budget, additional monies are unavailable. Current programs have been scrutinized rigidly and identifiable "fat" trimmed away. Thus high study costs are prohibitive at this time.

Lieutenant General Trudeau went on to state in a second letter, with the same date:

> It is considered of the utmost importance that the moon be first occupied by the US so that the US can deny Soviet territorial, commercial, or technological claims. If a permanent base can be established first by the United States, the prestige and psychological advantage to the nation will be invaluable.

Let's just assume for a moment that the cost was undeniably no issue. In addition, we will assume that the technological demand for launching all the needed supplies into orbit and constructing the base on the moon was also achievable. If all that was indeed possible, how would it all work? The Project Horizon research had it all figured out.

First and foremost, you need power. That power would come from nuclear power plants, constructed right there on the lunar surface by the advance team. After an outpost site was selected, craters were to be blasted into the lunar surface to make way for constructing these nuclear reactors. Yes, they were going to use explosives on the surface of the moon, to blast craters. Apparently, there are not enough craters on the moon already that they could have utilized, just to save a few bucks.

Second, you need a place to stay for the outpost crew, which was intended to initially total "nine men." As Volume 2 of the Project Horizon documents states:

> The lunar outpost facilities for the advance party, which will be used for housing during the construction of the main outpost, will consist of tank-type living quarters with utilities such as heat, light, air-conditioning and all the other interior essentials to provide an earthlike environment. The first two men and also the nine men in the advance party will live in the cabin of the vehicle in which they arrive until they have completed assembly of this advance outpost. It will be their goal to have the advance party quarters completed within 15 days after arrival of the nine-man construction crew. Maximum allowable time for this task is 30 days. Because of the importance of time and adverse environmental conditions, employment of special design and construction techniques is necessary. Three cargo-size tanks, pre-fabricated as living quarters, will be buried with at least three feet of lunar material coverage in a man-made trench. The excavation and backfill will be accomplished with a multi-purpose construction vehicle. These quarters will consist of one air-lock tank and two tanks for sleeping, dining and general living quarters.

Next up, would be the survivability of the crew, since not all the food and water could be brought with them. The water portion of their necessity would be in the form of a three-quarts-per-day ration. They would save water by salvaging what appeared in the atmosphere, and once condensed and collected, it would be used for washing, therefore reducing the need for additional water in excess of the drinking amount. They even had plans to reclaim the water portion of the astronauts' urine, which was to be saved by the crew, and that too was to be used within the outpost.

Food was another challenge. A four-pound per-man, per-day ration was planned. Food was sent prepackaged and precooked, separated into individual portions. Later plans involved utilizing algae grown at the outpost, which they aimed to develop the means to do so once the base was fully established. Hydroponics was also going to be used to grow the ingredients for salads, which according to the plan, had "morale values." Chickens and other poultry were on the agenda since they thrived in confined areas, they could eat the plant waste, and they would produce fresh eggs and provide meat.

Once the details about the necessities for survival were ironed out, of course, you needed to plan the machinery that would assist in the overall master plan. That included a "multi-purpose construction vehicle." Think of the lunar rover that history shows us from Apollo—and then feed it some steroids. Volume 2 offers the details on the pumped-up lunar rover:

> The vehicle is capable of performing general construction work to include the moving of lunar material, excavation of sub-surface trenches, heavy cargo handling, prime mover functions, and other mechanical work which man alone in a lunar suit cannot perform. To increase its heavy duty work potential, the light weight vehicle (4,500 pounds), will be ballastable up to twice its empty weight. It will be powered by two 4hp electric motors, one at each rear wheel. Electric power will be generated by a fuel cell installed directly over the rear axle. The vehicle will be self-loading by means of a dirt bowl located between the front and rear axle. The wheels will be all metal and four feet in diameter with 1½-inch diamond shaped grousers to improve traction. The vehicle will be approximately 15 feet long, six feet wide and six feet high. It will be capable of being operated remotely by control transmission cables or radio. A removable pressurized cab will be provided for the operator so he may work without a full lunar suit.
>
> The vehicle will be capable of a speed range up to 1½ mph for heavy duty work and up to 5 mph for cross country operation. Attachments will include fork lift arms, rooter teeth, "U" dozer blade, winch, crane boom and power take-off for other components such as a ground auger.

And last worth a mention, is that lunar suit mentioned in the previous excerpt. When Project Horizon was developed, man had yet to even land on the moon, and the suit for the Apollo program was not finalized. So, the US Army designed their own, which is nothing short of a page out of a science fiction book.

The document goes into great depth on what the suit would entail. Here is a summary of the "essential" elements:

1. Underwear: cotton undershirt; woolen cushion-sole socks; light impermeable urine and feces containers; cotton undershorts; modified for compatibility with sanitary containers.

Figure 8.3. A depiction of a "Lunar Construction Vehicle" is displayed in one of the released documents on the program. *Credit*: US Army

2. Main Suit: outer metal layer; inner anti-bremsstrahlung [electromagnetic radiation] metallic layer; self-sealant, cushioning, impermeable inner lining; flexible shoulder, elbow, hip, and knee joints; artificial hand operable by controls inside extremities of suit arms; transparent face piece; three-section construction—helmet, cuirass [armor], trousers—the latter two separable into halves; insulative dust shoes.

3. Thermal, respiratory and communications systems required: Back pack containing compressor, expansion coils, suit air pump, suit compressed air tank, oxygen tank, respiratory pump, CO_2 absorber, power source; radiative heat exchanger with connections to AC system; internal air distribution system; oxygen mask with connections to external system and external trip to lift the mask as required; communications antenna integrated into radiative heat exchanger.

Although there was detail that outlined nearly every facet of a lunar outpost, the idea stayed just that: an idea. As the Apollo program would unfold throughout the next decade, amazing strides were taken in the pursuit of

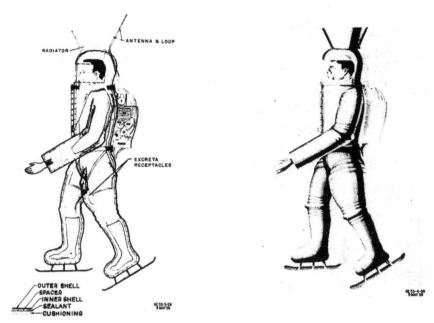

Figure 8.4.   Within the report, a "Lunar Suit" is designed for use. This was laid out prior to the implementation of the Apollo-era space suits and was likely just an idea and not a final proposal. *Credit*: US Army

science and human's goal of conquering space. However, a lunar outpost was just not part of that.

Yet, unbeknownst to the US Army, at the time they were designing a lunar base, the US Air Force was planning a much more dangerous plan within their own secret space agenda. As the US Army aimed to utilize the lunar surface and colonize it in a small way with an outpost, the US Air Force just aimed to blow up the moon—with a nuclear bomb.

9

A NUCLEAR BOMB
ON THE MOON?

The "space race" demanded an enormous amount of effort to get man to set foot on the moon. The scientific pursuit of such a feat required tenacity, patience, passion, and money. However, behind the scenes, it was not only science that was the driving factor. It was also national security and dominance.

Space dominance would allow any country that would achieve it first unparalleled advantages over all others. So, in addition to the scientific experiments planned and questions aimed to be answered, the US Army was planning a military lunar outpost that would be a permanent structure on the surface of the moon.

Although the US Army's military outpost never came to fruition, that we know of, the US Air Force had a completely different plan that they had cooked up for our closest celestial body. They simply wanted to just blow it up—and blow it up big.

The plan, which was crafted at nearly the exact time as the lunar outpost plan by the US Army, was called Project A119. It was outlined in a June 19, 1959, paper entitled, "A Study of Lunar Research Flights," sponsored by the Research Directorate of the Air Force Special Weapons Center (AFSWC) located at Kirtland Air Force Base, New Mexico.

The AFSWC origins go back to the Manhattan Project during the beginning stages of nuclear bomb development. Although it has operated under various names, it was called the AFSWC from April 1, 1952, through April 1, 1976. The center remained inactive until the US Air Force reactivated the

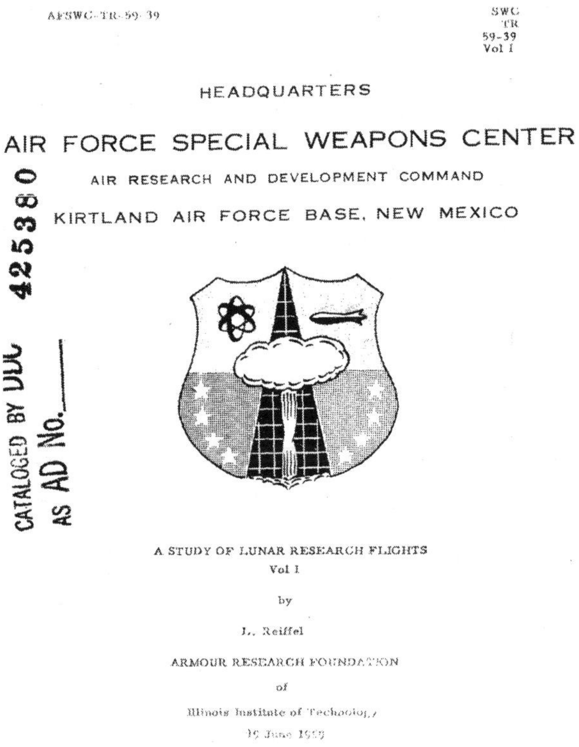

AFSWC-TR-59-39

SWC
TR
59-39
Vol I

HEADQUARTERS

AIR FORCE SPECIAL WEAPONS CENTER

AIR RESEARCH AND DEVELOPMENT COMMAND

KIRTLAND AIR FORCE BASE, NEW MEXICO

425380

CATALOGED BY DDC
AS AD No.

A STUDY OF LUNAR RESEARCH FLIGHTS
Vol I

by

L. Reiffel

ARMOUR RESEARCH FOUNDATION

of

Illinois Institute of Technology

19 June 1959

Figure 9.1. The cover page of "A Study of Lunar Research Flights," Volume I. *Credit*: US Army

unit on March 31, 2006, where it operates today under the name of the Air Force Nuclear Weapons Center.

It was during the operating years of the AFSWC that Project A119 was developed. A report was issued after the research was conducted that was authored by Leonard Reiffel, an American physicist, author, and educator. There was a short list of other contributors to the program, but one that sticks out on the cover page that most will recognize: C. E. Sagan. That's Carl Edward Sagan, famed astronomer and astrophysicist, and from the *Cosmos* fame. He was only twenty-four years old at the time this research was being conducted, and he played a key role in the understanding of the nuclear explosion in vacuum and low-gravity portion of the program.

The final report for the plan was "reviewed and approved" by Colonel Carey L. O'Bryan Jr. According to the abstract of the program's final report, it stated:

Nuclear detonations in the vicinity of the moon are considered in this report along with scientific information which might be obtained from such explosions. The military aspect is aided by investigation of space environment, detection of nuclear device testing, and capability of weapons in space.

A study was conducted of various theories of the moon's structure and origin, and a description of the probable nature of the lunar surface is given. The areas discussed in some detail are optical lunar studies, seismic observations, lunar surface and magnetic fields, plasma and magnetic field effects, and organic matter on the moon.

As with many other topics within this era of American history, it was feared and rumored that the Soviet Union was also planning a nuclear detonation on the moon. Since the Russians beat the Americans with the world's first satellite, which they called *Sputnik*, the United States knew that such a show of dominance by detonating a nuclear bomb on the moon would be a crushing defeat, should the Soviet Union achieve it. Whispers of them undertaking such a plan remained highly secretive at the time; however, a news story was published decades later by Russian online news agency Novinite, which ultimately confirmed the fear:

> The Soviet Union planned to blow up an atomic bomb on the Moon. This is clear from a secret document kept in the Russian State Archive, where journalists from the German TV Channel for historical broadcasting "Em De Er—Traveling in Time" have managed to get.
>
> According to the secret document of September 6, 1958, the Kremlin leadership issued a "top secret" order—in the summer of 1959 a Soviet atomic bomb would be blown up on the moon.

Although some may argue that Russian media, even post–Cold War, may not be trusted, Dr. Matthias Ul, a scientist at the German Historical Institute in Moscow, confirmed that the documents were true and the "Top Secret" Soviet order was authentic. So, it appears that even though the concept sounded crazy, there was a covert push by both nations to achieve it first.

The Russian equivalent to Project A119 was discovered to be a series of projects that start with the code name "E" and were numbered sequentially one through four. Project E-1 was the plan to reach the moon. Project E-2 and E-3 included sending a probe to the dark, or far side, of the moon to photograph the lunar surface and find a prime detonation epicenter. Project

E-4 was the final phase—the nuclear detonation on the moon. However, plans were scrapped by the Soviets and it never took place, presumably for the same reasons the Americans did not do the same thing. More on that later in this chapter.

Back to the American Project A119. The report made it clear that there were primarily three motivating factors for conducting such an experiment: scientific, military, and political. The scientific factor, which we will deal with first, was the most obvious. This endeavor would tie into the work of the contracted Armour Research Foundation (ARF), which was located at the Illinois Institute of Technology. The ARF had begun studying the effects of nuclear explosions throughout various environments, beginning in 1949. Then, secretly in May of 1958, the ARF began the research into the detonation of a nuclear weapon on the lunar surface that became known as Project A119, an idea first conceived and proposed by the US Air Force and then contracted to the ARF for further study.

Scientifically, a nuclear detonation on the moon could create a plume that could be used for analyzing the makeup of the lunar surface. However, a huge problem presents itself when using a nuclear bomb to analyze samples in the wake of the blast, and that would be the radiation that the bomb itself leaves behind. As the report outlines, the "natural radiation" of the lunar surface needs to be calculated *prior* to any nuclear detonation. This allows for any future readings to be able to differentiate between the normal radiation that exists on the moon and the numbers *after* a detonation, which will undoubtedly increase it. Additional analysis could also be done by the instrumentation utilized.

Once normal radiation levels are calculated, the contents of any plume generated from the blast could be analyzed, and a somewhat accurate composition of the moon's surface could be determined—minus the additional radiation of the blast. Although there were many scenarios that Project A119 laid out, the report summarizes the idea:

> In summary: when one considers the natural radiation at the lunar surface, it appears clear that fairly sophisticated instrumentation will be required to measure lunar radioactivity, for example, in the presence of natural interference. Without adding a great deal of complexity, such apparatus should be able to distinguish the modest lunar contamination produced from a nuclear burst near the moon's surface. Such a conclusion does not, of course, argue

for the casual detonation of a nuclear weapon near the moon, but it does appear that with instrumentation emplaced on the moon prior to such a detonation which would, in fact, be capable of making meaningful measurements, the influence of a subsequent nuclear detonation would not be as detrimental to the information content of the moon as is sometimes argued. Clearly, however, it will be to the advantage of any experiment to have data on the natural radiation before detonation of any device producing radioactivity. When such data are available our conclusions here should be reviewed carefully.

Aside from the science potential, militarily, Project A119 would allow the upper echelon of the US armed forces to see firsthand how a nuclear bomb performed in a space environment. Should the Cold War escalate to space warfare, this test would allow them to understand the true capability of a nuclear weapon, should that space warfare require the knowledge.

Lastly, and possibly the most important, was the political implications behind Project A119. This proposal would allow a show of force from high up into space. It was theorized that once detonated, the nuclear blast on the moon could be seen by the naked eye from Earth. This would serve a multitude of purposes, but primarily, it would show a dominance of space by the United States over the Soviet Union, and ultimately, the entire world.

To achieve maximum visibility, the plan proposed two factors. (1) The bomb would be detonated on the "terminator" of the moon: the area between where the lunar surface that is illuminated by the sun meets the area that is always dark. This is also called the "dark side of the moon." Detonating the bomb in that spot would ensure that the people of Earth, and its world leaders, would be able to detect it. (2) To maximize visibility when the bomb detonates, a "sodium cloud" would be created by adding sodium to the bombs. According to the report, here is why adding the element would be beneficial:

In 1955 US experiments with sodium vaporization in atmosphere up to an altitude of 30–40 kilometers were begun for studying winds at these altitudes and the chemical reactions of gases in these atmospheric layers with sodium. On January 3, 1959, the Russians set a cloud formed of the sodium vapors in an atomic state. The sodium cloud is discharged at a specified moment and it glows because of resonance fluorescence emitting the sodium lines. The yellow light is preferred from the point of view of visual sensitivity. Furthermore, use of narrow band interference filters can enhance the contrast.

The brilliance of sodium cloud containing one kilogram of sodium and discharged 113,000 kms away from the earth is equal to a sixth magnitude star which is at the threshold of naked eye visibility against average sky background.

Of course, such an elaborate plan would not come without consequences. Volume I of "A Study of Lunar Research Flights" explored the organic matter on the moon and possible effects on it all should they detonate a nuclear blast.

Since the deposition of an instrumented package on the lunar surface is implicit in many of the experiments discussed in the report as well as being imminent as a result of other US or Russian activities, there has been considerable recent concern that terrestrial organisms and organic matter, deposited with the package, may obscure detection of possible organisms or organic matter indigenous to the moon. If such a biological contamination of the moon occurred, it would represent an unparalleled scientific disaster, eliminating several possibly very fruitful approaches to such problems as the early history of the solar system, the chemical composition of matter in the remote past, the origin of life on earth, and the possibility of extraterrestrial life. Because of the moon's unique situation as a large unweathered body in the middle of the solar system, scientific opportunities lost on the moon may not be recouped elsewhere. Accordingly, it is of interest to determine (a) the survival probability of a terrestrial life-form on the moon, and (b) the possibility that organic matter was produced during the previous history of the moon, has survived to the present epoch, and could be confused with the remains of contemporary terrestrial life-forms.

We know that the plan, again as far as we know, was never carried out by the United States or by Russia, and we can safely assume the latter did not do it for the same reasons the Americans didn't. However, there is a lot to the puzzle that is missing, which is worthy of note. Recall earlier in the chapter I mentioned a young Dr. Sagan who played a role in the study? Well, it is believed that Dr. Sagan himself was the one that blew the cover on this elaborate plan to detonate a nuclear bomb on the moon, when the US military likely did not want the project known at all.

It ties back to the creation of Dr. Sagan's biography, written by Keay Davidson, entitled, *Carl Sagan: A Life*. In the course of writing this book, Davidson had outlined some not-so-flattering details about Sagan and his pursuit of trying to make it while he was still very young in his career. The biography detailed the fact that Sagan may have knowingly revealed classified information in order to increase his chances of winning a Miller Institute graduate fellowship to Berkeley in 1959. Although Sagan had the support of Nobelist H. J. Muller, who said Sagan, "stood head and shoulders above" the rest of the candidates, Davidson claimed that it may not have been enough for Sagan. So, it was asserted by the author of his biography that Sagan revealed classified information for the judges to take note of his work. Davidson writes:

> [Sagan] decided to confide to [the fellowship judges] information that he was required by federal law to keep secret. He revealed his research at the Armour Research Foundation on the remote detection of lunar nuclear explosions. He must have known the risk he was taking. The information was classified; he had previously cautioned Muller not to discuss it with others. . . . Washington did not look kindly on the leaking of nuclear information.

I will be clear that the allegation has never been fully substantiated, but when *Nature, International Journal of Science* published the review of *Carl Sagan: A Life*, they detailed this story. As a result, Freedom of Information Act (FOIA) requests were filed, and Volume I of "A Study of Lunar Research Flights" was discovered and released to the public. The claims in regard to Sagan's involvement in the plans for detonating a nuclear bomb on the moon were substantiated.

This led to immediate media coverage about the secret plan, which included the *New York Times* in 2000. They tracked down Reiffel, who authored the Project A119 study, and they questioned him about the claim of Sagan potentially revealing classified information. Although some book reviewers disagreed with Davidson's assertion that Sagan revealed classified information, Reiffel agreed with it. In support of the fact that the information should have remained a secret, Reiffel stated, "I wanted to set the record straight. There would have been an outcry if the project had been made public."

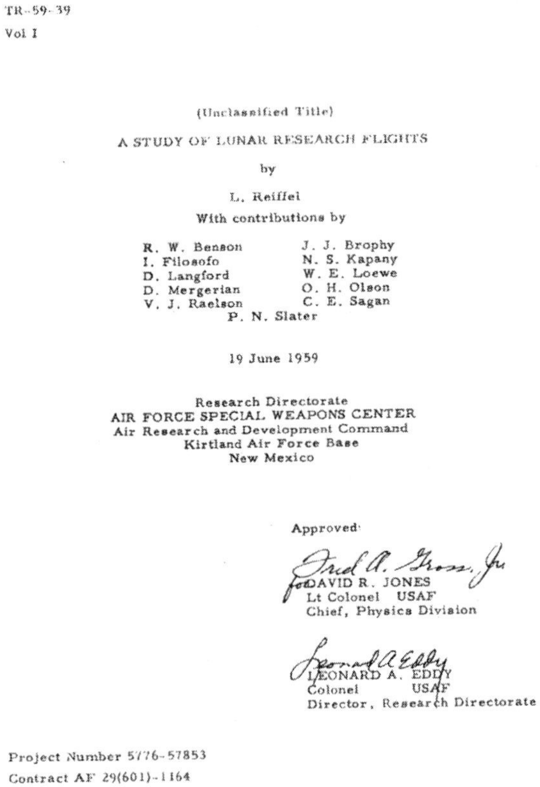

TR-59-39
Vol I

(Unclassified Title)

A STUDY OF LUNAR RESEARCH FLIGHTS

by

L. Reiffel

With contributions by

R. W. Benson   J. J. Brophy
I. Filosofo   N. S. Kapany
D. Langford   W. E. Loewe
D. Mergerian   O. H. Olson
V. J. Raelson   C. E. Sagan
P. N. Slater

19 June 1959

Research Directorate
AIR FORCE SPECIAL WEAPONS CENTER
Air Research and Development Command
Kirtland Air Force Base
New Mexico

Figure 9.2. On the list of contributors appeared a scientist by the name of C. E. Sagan, or Carl Sagan, of the *Cosmos* television series fame. *Credit*: Department of Defense (DOD)

Approved:

DAVID R. JONES
Lt Colonel USAF
Chief, Physics Division

LEONARD A. EDDY
Colonel   USAF
Director, Research Directorate

Project Number 5776-57853
Contract AF 29(601)-1164

Another interesting factoid revealed itself once Volume I of the study was officially released: an untold amount of information was missing or destroyed. Usually when you find something which says, "Volume I," you can easily deduce there is at least a "Volume II," if not more. In its "Table of Contents," Volume II is even referenced to contain Volume I's chapters II and IX, which is an odd, and unexplained, point as well. Normally, you would have all chapters of a volume in that very volume—you wouldn't put random entire chapters in another volume. It defeats the purpose of having multiple volumes, commonly split to differentiate between different angles on the topic or to break up large sections. These chapters also remain title-less, so it is impossible to understand what they deal with.

This, of course, begs to ask the question, "Where is Volume II?" Sadly, nowhere to be found. Many researchers, including myself, have aimed to find Volume II, and verify if any additional volumes exist. It appears they have been destroyed, and whatever Volume I's chapters II and IX contained have also been lost.

Despite Project A119 never taking place, a future NASA mission that journeyed into space on June 18, 2009, had eerie similarities to the scientific aspect of the proposed nuclear detonation on the lunar surface.

The Lunar Crater Observation and Sensing Satellite, or LCROSS, roared its way from Space Launch Complex Forty-One, Cape Canaveral, Florida, to the moon. The LCROSS spacecraft aimed to determine the nature of hydrogen detected at the polar regions of Earth's moon.

After India had launched its first lunar probe called *Chandrayaan-1*, the mission had discovered a widespread presence of water molecules within the lunar soil of its polar region. This prompted NASA to create the LCROSS mission in order to confirm the findings and collect additional data for analysis. NASA's original press packet for LCROSS explained the mission:

> LCROSS is a spectacular mission that is taking a novel approach at answering a lingering scientific question: does water ice exist on the moon? If the answer is yes, it could potentially be a useful resource for future exploration. LCROSS represents a new generation of fast development, cost-capped missions that use off-the-shelf hardware and flight-proven software to achieve focused mission goals. LCROSS also uses the spent second stage of the Atlas rocket, the Centaur, as an SUV-sized kinetic impactor—something that has never been done before—to excavate a small crater in the bottom of a permanently shadowed lunar crater.
>
> Whatever LCROSS discovers about the presence of water, it will increase our knowledge of the mineralogical makeup of some of the most remote areas of the moon—deep polar craters where sunshine never reaches. People around the world will take part in observation campaigns to witness the mission's historic twin impacts on the lunar surface and their results.
>
> These companion missions, launched together on an Atlas V rocket, will mark the return of NASA to the moon and usher in a new era of scientific exploration of our sister in the solar system.

For the most part, LCROSS was a success. Regardless of a malfunction that depleted most of the fuel for the LCROSS mission, it was able to achieve impact with the Centaur stage of the Atlas rocket. At more than fifty-five hundred miles an hour, Centaur impacted the Cabeus crater successfully, releasing an energy equivalent to two tons of TNT. Although that is a far cry from the one thousand tons of TNT released from a nuclear kiloton bomb, or the one million tons in a megaton bomb, it showed the theory that an explosion on the surface of the moon could yield viable scientific results.

There is no documented connection between the Project A119 proposal of blowing up the surface of the moon with a nuclear bomb in 1959 and the LCROSS/Centaur mission aimed to create an explosion on the surface in 2009. However, details of both plans show that no matter how crazy an idea may seem—program elements may find themselves in similar scientific endeavors fifty years after the idea is conceived.

10

EYES IN THE SKY

From Mercury, Gemini, and then through Apollo, the missions within the space program of the United States accomplished many scientific feats. Mercury's aim was to understand how a human could function in space and be brought back to Earth safely. Gemini aimed toward, and achieved, researching various methods for space travel, and perfected the techniques to take man to the moon. Apollo's mission was to land on our closest celestial neighbor and learn everything we could about it.

Behind the scenes, there were various aspects to these programs that were much more sinister in nature, like blowing up the moon with a nuclear weapon, or building a military space outpost to ensure dominance on the lunar surface. Yet, in addition to all that, another program within the space program would remain classified for decades: the Corona satellite.

THE CORONA PROGRAM

Corona was a reconnaissance satellite that was operated by the CIA beginning in June of 1959 and lasting until May of 1972. Although it was ultimately a CIA-run program, the US Air Force also played a large part in assisting with launches and other aspects to the program.

The main goal of Corona was to capture photographic surveillance primarily of the Soviet Union and of China. Due to these objectives, secrecy was paramount when dealing with the Corona program. In a declassified, formerly "Top Secret" memorandum dated May 12, 1959, Deputy Director (Intelligence) Robert Amory Jr. writes the following:

1. The following proposal for the exploitation of information derived from Project CORONA is based on the following assumptions:

   a. Security will place strict limitations on the numbers of people that can work on and have access to information produced by Project CORONA.
   b. At some point about one year or 18 months after the initiation of Project CORONA, developments in the SENTRY Program will probably make it possible to reduce the classification of CORONA derived material making it available to the Intelligence Community on a fairly liberal basis.
   c. As a result of the strict security, and the fact that the need for security will probably be reduced within a fairly definite period of time, there will be no large scale program to sanitize CORONA material.

The memorandum went on to detail the limited number of people who could know about the program. By the way the memorandum reads, it was going to stay a relatively small number of people, however, even to this day, the exact number of "Corona Clearances" that were granted to various offices remains classified.

Despite the immense secrecy involved around the program, there are records that have been declassified that shed light on the scope of the actual program. In one declassified, formerly "Top Secret," CIA document entitled, "A Century of Corona," the origins of the program are outlined in detail:

When the U-2 Program first got under way, it was anticipated that in one to one and one-half years the Soviets would be able to counter with a surface-to-air missile. It was anticipated, however, that within this period SAMOS would take over the photo reconnaissance collection. However, because of SAMOS development difficulties, the White House approved the development of a satellite-borne camera and recoverable capsule, the beginning of the CORONA reconnaissance program in April 1958.

The CORONA Program was carried out under the authority of CIA and the Advanced Research Projects Agency (ARPA) with support of the Air Force. Booster proposal work in early feasibility investigations had been performed earlier as part of Air Force Weapons System 117L (Sentry). The CIA was charged with the development of the reconnaissance equipment,

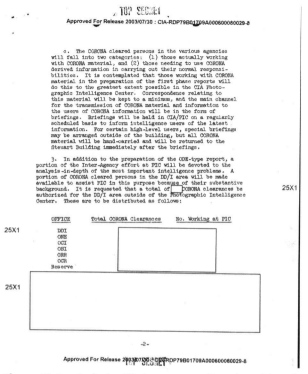

Figure 10.1. A declassified page revealing that although the page was released to the public, the number of those cleared for the Corona program was considered still classified. *Credit*: Central Intelligence Agency (CIA)

security, cover, covert procurement, and collection requirements. In behalf of ARPA, the Air Force contracted for and directed the detailed procurements on the overt side. These included the booster, the AGENA 2nd stage, control networks, launch facilities, and the basic recovery vehicle development.

The Corona program, although ultimately a success, did not start off as such. On January 21, 1959, the first launch of the Corona program was going to take place at Vandenberg Air Force Base. As the rocket was being loaded with fuel, a test of the launch computer sequencer was initiated. This resulted in the Agena booster receiving a signal to separate the main booster, and the rocket began a sequence that would cripple it as it was still on the launchpad. Although someone on the launchpad was able to press an emergency shutdown button, and absolute disaster was averted, this was a major setback that was supposed to be the first launch of the program.

In addition to this, the CIA's *CORONA: America's First Satellite Program* further explains the obstacles the program needed to overcome:

> The test plan contemplated arriving at full operational capability at a relatively early date through sequential testing of the major components of the system beginning with the THOR-AGENA combination alone, then adding the nose cone to test the ejection/re-entry/recovery sequence, and finally installing a camera for a full CORONA systems test. Just how much confidence the project planners had in the imminence of success cannot now be discovered; however, if the confidence factor was very high at the start it must soon have begun to wane. Beginning in February 1959 and extending through June 1960 an even dozen launches were attempted, with eight of the vehicles carrying cameras, and all of them were failures; no film capsules were recovered from orbit. Of the eight camera-carrying vehicles, four failed to achieve orbit, three experienced camera or film failures, and the eighth was not recovered because of a malfunction of the re-entry body spin rockets. These summaries of the initial launch attempts illustrate the nature and dimensions of the problems for which solutions had to be found.

One of the more interesting aspects to the Corona program was the recovery of the film cannister. In the twenty-first-century world, data is transmitted wirelessly. Even from the surface of another planet, like Mars, NASA will receive reams of photographs wirelessly, as beamed from the surface of the red planet. However, in the 1960s, technology was much different, and photographs were taken on film.

So, how would analysts cleared to see the photographs back on Earth obtain them? The CIA's *CORONA: America's First Satellite Program* outlines the incredible details on how this was to be achieved. And in order to do it, it had to be "perfect":

> The planned recovery sequence involved a series of maneuvers, each of which had to be executed to near-perfection or recovery would fail. Immediately after injection into orbit, the AGENA vehicle was yawed 180 degrees so that the recovery vehicle faced to the rear. This maneuver [minimized] the control gas which would be required for re-entry orientation at the end of the mission, and protected the heat shield from molecular heating, a

Figure 10.2.   Undated image of an Air Force C-119 recovering a Corona film canister as it returns to Earth from space. *Credit*: US Army

subject of considerable concern at that time. (Later in the J-3 design when these concerns had diminished, the vehicle would be flown forward until re-entry.) When re-entry was to take place, the AGENA would then be pitched down through 60 degrees to position the satellite recovery vehicle (SRV) for retro-firing. Then the SRV would be separated from the AGENA and be spin-stabilized by firing the spin rockets to maintain it in the attitude given it by the AGENA. Next the retro-rocket would be fired, slowing down the SRV into a descent trajectory. Then the spin of the SRV would be slowed by firing the de-spin rockets. Next would come the separation of the retro-rocket thrust cone followed by the heat shield and the parachute cover. The drogue (or deceleration) chute would then deploy, and finally the main chute would open to lower the capsule gently into the recovery area. The primary recovery technique involved flying an airplane across the top of the descending parachute, catching the chute or its shrouds in a trapeze-like hook suspended beneath the airplane and then winching the recovery vehicle aboard. C-119 Aircraft were initially used with C-130 aircraft replacing them later in the program. The recovery vehicle was designed to float long enough, if the air catch failed, for a water recovery by helicopter launched from a surface ship.

It is quite amazing that the film cannister could be recovered at all, with such an immense number of variables that had to go to "perfection" in order to be achieved. Yet, despite the overwhelming odds that such a plan would even work, it did. A 2016 US Army article, written by Sharon Watkins Lang (SMDC/ARSTRAST Command Historian) about the program explains:

> The next major accomplishments for Discoverer/Corona came in August 1960. Launched from Vandenberg Air Force Base atop a Thor-Agena rocket the Corona/Discoverer XIII completed 17 orbits of the Earth. On Aug. 12, 1960, this capsule, which was not equipped with a camera, became the first man-made object recovered from an orbiting satellite. An American flag flown in space aboard the capsule was later presented to President Dwight Eisenhower in a ceremony at the Oval Office.
>
> Six days later came the first fully successful Corona mission. On Aug. 18, 1960, a Corona capsule was launched into space and orbited the Earth for a day. On the next day, the Air Force achieved a mid-air recovery of the Corona XIV capsule with its camera (KH-1) and 20-pounds of film, the first detailed photographic images from space. Flight XIV covered more than 1,650,000 square miles of Soviet territory and produced more images than all of the earlier U-2 missions combined. The age of satellite reconnaissance had begun.

Despite a rough start, with each success as the program went on, additional strides and upgrades were achieved, making Corona a viable part in aerial reconnaissance at the time. Within the program, there were multiple missions and satellites launched, which then paved the way for additional missions. The CIA's *CORONA: America's First Satellite Program* outlines the first of the Corona satellites:

> The first four versions of CORONA were designated RX-1 through KH-4 (KH denoted KEYHOLE); KH-4 went through three versions. The camera in KH-l—public cover name DISCOVERER—had a nominal ground resolution of 40 feet. (Ground resolution is the ground size equivalent of the smallest visible imagery and its associated space.) By 1963 improvements to the original CORONA had produced the KH-2 and KH-3, with cameras that achieved resolutions of 10 feet.
>
> The first ISIS-4 mission was launched in 1962 and brought a major breakthrough in technology by using the MURAL camera to provide stereoscopic imagery. This meant that two cameras photographed each target from dif-

ferent angles, which allowed imagery analysts to look at KH-4 stereoscopic photos as three-dimensional. In the KH-4, the workhorse of the CORONA system, three camera models with different resolutions were the principal difference between the versions, KH-4, KII-4A, and RI-I-4B. By 1967, the J-3 camera of KH-4B had entered service with a resolution of 5 feet. This final version of CORONA continued overflights until 1972.

That same year is when the CIA's History Staff within their Center for the Study of Intelligence published *CORONA: America's First Satellite Program*. Within that text, the Corona program, despite its hardships, was largely labeled a success:

CORONA's initial major accomplishment was imaging all Soviet medium-range, intermediate-range, and intercontinental ballistic missile launching complexes. CORONA also identified the Plesetsk Missile Test Range, north of Moscow. Repetitive coverage of centers like Plesetsk provided information as to what missiles were being developed, tested, and/or deployed. Also, the unequivocal fact of observation gave the United States freedom from concern over many areas and locations which had been suspect in the past.

Severodvinsk, the main Soviet construction site for ballistic-missile-carrying submarines was first seen by CORONA. Now it was possible to monitor the launching of each new class of submarines and follow it through deployment to operational bases. Similarly, one could observe Soviet construction and deployment of the ocean-going surface fleet.

Coverage of aircraft factories and airbases provided an inventory of bomber and fighter forces. Great strides were also made in compiling an improved Soviet ground order of battle.

It was CORONA imagery which uncovered Soviet antiballistic missile activity. Construction of the GALOSH sites around Moscow and the GRIF-FON site near Leningrad, together with construction of sites around Tallinn for the Soviet surface-to-air missile known as the SA-5, were first observed in CORONA imagery.

HEN HOUSE, DOG HOUSE, and the Soviet Union's first phased-array radars—all associated with the Soviet ABM program—were also identified in CORONA imagery.

CORONA "take" was also used to locate Soviet SA-1 and SA-2 installations; later its imagery was used to find SA-3 and SA-5 batteries. The precise location of these defenses provided Strategic Air Command planners with the information needed to determine good entry and egress routes for US strategic bombers.

CORONA imagery was also adapted extensively to serve the needs of the Army Map Service and its successor, the Defense Mapping Agency (DMA). Enhanced by improvements in system attitude control and ephemeris data plus the addition of a stellar-index camera, CORONA eventually became almost the sole source of DMKs military mapping data.

In another document declassified in 2010 by the National Reconnaissance Office (NRO), entitled "The Corona Story," the NRO offers even more information on Corona's success:

The CIA described the CORONA contribution to US intelligence holdings as "virtually immeasurable." By June 1964, CORONA had delivered photos of every Soviet ICBM complex in existence; using these data as a benchmark, the United States was in a position to follow the course of Soviet buildup, item by item. CORONA provided priceless coverage of the Middle East during the 1967 War and in 1970 was used to test Israeli-Egyptian claims regarding cease-fire compliance.

The Corona program remained classified for decades, and it was not declassified until 1995 when President Bill Clinton signed Executive Order (EO) 12951, which declassified imagery acquired by space-based reconnaissance systems. Not only the Corona program, but other highly classified programs such as Argon and Lanyard were named in the order for declassification.

BEYOND CORONA

President Clinton's EO introduced additional program names that, although connected by lineage to the Corona program, identified them as offshoot programs and systems. The Argon missions, which had launches from 1961 through 1964, was designated the KH-5, and was very similar to the way Corona operated with a film ejection method for data recovery. In total, there were at least twelve missions for Argon; however, there are seven known failures. Despite some information released and declassified, there is still much withheld on the exact number of launches, missions, successes, and failures.

President Clinton's EO 12951 also revealed that information relating to Lanyard would be declassified, which was named the KH-6. The 1963 mission was unsuccessful, but it served as the first high-resolution optical reconnaissance satellite launched by the National Reconnaissance Office (NRO).

There were three launches within the Lanyard program. One was a total failure; another had no film; and the third was able to achieve orbit with film, and the result was considered a success, but the result was far from meeting the objective. The Lanyard program was cancelled after this specific mission. A NASA fact sheet relating to this mission outlines what went wrong:

This US Air Force surveillance satellite was launched from Vandenberg AFB aboard a Thor Agena D rocket. This was the third and final KH-6 (LAN-YARD) mission that was designed to provide very high [resolution] photos (2'), but the best resolution achieved was 6', the same as KH-4B, so LAN-YARD was [discontinued] after this 3rd flight in 1963. The initial stimulus for this added resolution was suspected ABM sites around Leningrad.

The camera failed after 32 hours. The mission was deemed a success but the image quality was poor.

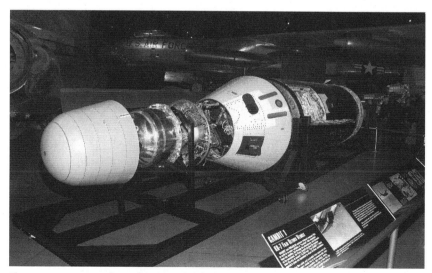

Figure 10.3.   Here is a photograph of the Gambit 1 KH-7, one of three formerly classified reconnaissance satellites that went on display at the National Museum of the US Air Force in Dayton, Ohio. *Credit*: US Air Force

The Gambit program operated from July 1963 through June 1967 and included the KH-7 and KH-8. An NRO "fact sheet" on the program describes the major differences between Gambit and the earlier Corona programs:

Although Corona provided the capability to search large areas from space, the US still lacked high resolution imagery. Approximately one year after the first launch of Corona, the National Reconnaissance Office began development of its first high resolution satellite program, code-named Gambit. Over time, the Gambit program evolved into two different systems. The first Gambit system, launched in 1963, was equipped with the KH-7 camera system that included a 77-inch focal length camera for providing specific information on scientific and technical capabilities that threatened the nation. Intelligence users often characterized this capability as surveillance, allowing the United States to track the advancement of Soviet and others' capabilities. The second system, Gambit 3 was equipped with the KH-8 camera system that included a 175-inch focal length camera. The system was first launched in 1966 and provided the US with exquisite surveillance capabilities from space for nearly two decades. The NRO launched a final system, code-named Hexagon, in 1971 to improve upon Corona's capability to search broad and wide denied areas for threats to the United States. The system sometimes carried a mapping camera to aid in US military war planning. The United States depended on these search and surveillance satellites to understand the capabilities, intentions, and advancements of those who opposed the United States during the Cold War. Together they became America's essential eyes in space.

The Hexagon program, or KH-9, operated from June 1971 through April 1986. There were twenty Hexagon launches within that time frame. Now declassified, the United States Air Force Museum, located at Wright-Patterson Air Force Base, displays a KH-9. They also offer details about the program:

HEXAGON KH-9 reconnaissance satellites were the largest and last US intelligence satellites to return photographic film to earth. During the Cold War, 19 HEXAGON missions imaged 877 million square miles of the Earth's surface between 1971–1986.

HEXAGON's main purpose was wide-area search. Analysts pored over HEXAGON's photos of large areas, then focused in on potential threats with close-up surveillance from GAMBIT satellites.

The Lockheed Corp. built the HEXAGON vehicle. Its development included creating a very complex camera and film system. The satellite featured two separate cameras, designated KH-9 and made by the Perkin-Elmer Corp., working together to produce stereo images. These so-called "optical bar cameras" on the bottom of the satellite spun on their axes, taking overlapping images to form a very large panoramic picture. Objects smaller than two feet across could be imaged from around 80–100 miles altitude.

Some missions included a separate mapping camera mounted at the front of the satellite. This camera imaged wider areas to make very accurate maps for war planning and featured its own bucket-like film return vehicle.

The US Air Force launched HEXAGON satellites aboard Titan IIID rockets from Vandenberg AFB, California, and provided tracking and control at an Air Force facility at Sunnyvale, Calif. USAF aircraft recovered film return vehicles in midair near Hawaii.

THE KH-10 AND THE MANNED ORBITAL LABORATORY (MOL)

The KH-10, or DORIAN, introduced a new level of satellite-based reconnaissance. It began researching the concept of putting man above the Earth for military surveillance. So, instead of satellites taking pictures, and ejecting film canisters back to Earth for recovery, the KH-10 missions would equip a larger US Air Force–led program known as the Manned Orbital Laboratory (later renamed the Manned Orbiting Laboratory [MOL]).

Surprisingly, the MOL was publicly acknowledged, even back in 1964 when it began. However, what makes the MOL so interesting is that there was a much more secretive aspect to the program that was not explained in their initial announcement.

Publicly, the MOL was announced on December 10, 1964. The Department of Defense (DOD) issued the following press statement:

> Secretary of Defense Robert S. McNamara today assigned to the Air Force a new program for the development of a near earth Manned Orbiting Laboratory (MOL).
>
> The MOL program, which will consist of an orbiting pressurized cylinder approximately the size of a small house trailer, will increase the Defense Department effort to determine military usefulness of man in space. This pro-

gram, while increasing this effort, will permit savings of approximately $100 million over present 1964–1965 military space programmed expenditures.

MOL will be designed so that astronauts can move about freely in it without a space suit and conduct observations and experiments in the laboratory over a period of up to a month. The first manned flight of the MOL is expected late in 1967 or early in 1968.

In initiating the MOL program, it was decided to terminate the DYNA-SOAR (X-20) program because the current requirement is for a program aimed directly at the basic question of man's utility in space, rather than a program limited to finding means to control the return of man from space. The DYNASOAR project was designed to do the latter.

The DYNASOAR vehicle is a one-man spacecraft, launched from a TI-TAN III booster. It was designed to test the feasibility of maneuverability during reentry, thus allowing the pilot to choose a landing site and land in a manner similar to a conventional aircraft.

The MOL will be attached to a modified GEMINI capsule and lifted into orbit by a TITAN III booster. The GEMINI capsule is being developed by NASA for use in the APOLLO moon shot program. The TITAN III is being developed as a standardized space booster by the Air Force.

Astronauts will be seated in the modified GEMINI capsule during launch and will move to the laboratory after injection into orbit. After completion of their tasks in space, the astronauts will return to the capsule, which will then be detached from the laboratory to return to earth.

The design of the MOL vehicle will permit rendezvous in space between the orbiting laboratory and a second GEMINI capsule, so that relief crews could replace original crews in the laboratory. Such an operation would be undertaken if man's utility in a space environment were demonstrated and long operations in the space laboratory were needed.

The MOL program will make use of the existing NASA control facilities. These include the tracking facilities which have been set up for the GEMINI and other space flight programs of NASA and of the Department of Defense throughout the world.

The laboratory itself will conduct military experiments involving manned use of equipment and instrumentation in orbit and, if desired by NASA, for scientific and civilian purposes. Preliminary ground or aircraft simulation will be made in all cases before full commitment to space experimentation.

The problem of reentry conditions, materials and techniques can be studied at substantially lower costs without actually using a manned vehicle like DYNASOAR. The MOL program will permit much more extensive

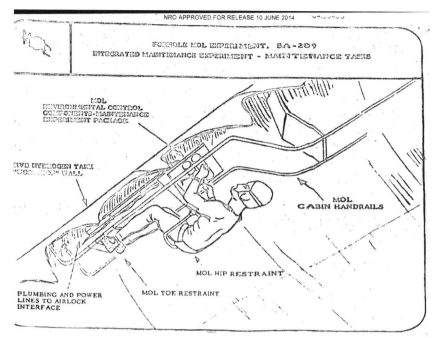

NRO APPROVED FOR RELEASE 10 JUNE 2014

POSSIBLE MOL EXPERIMENT. SA-209
INTEGRATED MAINTENANCE EXPERIMENT - MAINTENANCE TASKS

MOL
ENVIRONMENTAL CONTROL
COMPONENTS-MAINTENANCE
EXPERIMENT PACKAGE

RVD HYDROGEN TANK
"WORKSHOP" WALL

MOL
CABIN HANDRAILS

MOL HIP RESTRAINT

PLUMBING AND POWER
LINES TO AIRLOCK
INTERFACE

MOL TOE RESTRAINT

Figure 10.4. A declassified page from the National Reconnaissance Office (NRO) files depicting a section of the Manned Orbiting Laboratory (MOL) with an astronaut inside. *Credit*: National Reconnaissance Office (NRO)

exploration of the in-flight capabilities of the manned space vehicle. If results of the MOL and the unmanned reentry programs warrant, a new and more advanced ferry vehicle program may be initiated some years in the future.

Yet, as mentioned, the public version of the MOL was much different from the actual mission. After its declassification, the NRO offers the following describing the MOL:

The Manned Orbiting Laboratory (MOL) was a 1960s Air Force program with the ostensible mission to place military personnel in orbit to conduct scientific experiments to determine the "military usefulness" of placing man into space and the techniques and procedures for doing so if the need ever arose. The actual, classified, mission of the MOL program was to place a manned surveillance satellite into orbit. At the time, several military and contractor studies estimated that manned surveillance satellites could acquire photographic coverage of the Soviet Union with resolution better than the best system at the time (the first-generation Gambit satellite). Additionally, the Air Force billed the MOL as a reconnaissance system that could more efficiently and quickly adjust coverage for crises and targets of opportunity than unmanned systems. The Air Force controlled development of the satellite, which was consistent with MOL's unclassified mission, while the NRO ran development of the covert reconnaissance mission of the program, including the camera system and other subsystems.

Secretary of Defense McNamara publicly announced the start of the MOL program in December 1963. However, even though the program had support from the military and the President, it was seldom fully funded due to competition from other DoD programs, NASA, and general governmental budgetary pressure. By the time initial studies, planning, and organization were completed and the program was ready to expand into full-scale development and production in the late-60s, budgetary pressure had significantly increased due to NASA's Apollo program and the Vietnam War. At a time when the program required increased expenditures, its budget was being slashed, and as a result, its timelines and costs were expanded and increased. With growing pressure from the expansion of the Vietnam War, the perceived duplication of effort with NASA programs, and improved performance of operating unmanned surveillance systems, in June 1969 the President cancelled the MOL program, and with it, the Air Force's last chance to develop a manned space flight program. The MOL program operated for five and one half years and spent $1.56 billion, but never launched a manned vehicle into space.

The MOL was canceled due to the budgetary constraints and realization that unmanned reconnaissance stations were much cheaper, and had much less risk. The advancement to the next generation KH-11 or Kennen, also allowed for the realization that unmanned vehicles were the way to go.

The KH-11 was first launched in December of 1976 and was later renamed to CRYSTAL in 1982, adopting the designation of KH-12. Originally designed by Lockheed-Martin, it was the first spy satellite of its kind to use "electro-optical digital imaging," which allowed for a real-time, optical observation. The days of film cannister retrievals were over.

The KH-11 and the KH-12 also introduced a new launch system, unlike the missions prior. Up until this point, going back to the original Corona launches, all were launched by multistaged rockets, including the THOR-AGENA, the ATLAS-AGENA, the TITAN-III, and the TITAN

34D. However, the KH-11 and the KH-12 were different. These would be launched into space via a new vehicle in use by NASA—the space shuttle.

On February 28, 1990, the space shuttle *Atlantis* roared from Kennedy Space Center Launch Complex 39 on its way to space. Hidden within the cargo was a classified payload designated 1990-019B. It is believed that this designation was an advanced KH-11 that the Department of Defense piggybacked on the shuttle mission for launch of their satellite. NASA explains this portion of NASA's mission STS-36.

KH 11-10 was deployed from the orbiting STS-36 for the US Department of Defense. It was an electro-optical [reconnaissance] satellite that was heavier than other KH-11 satellites and believed to include a signals intelligence payload. It had wider spectral band sensitivity, perhaps "real time" television capability, and other improvements compared to the other KH-11 satellites. The satellite was reported to have malfunctioned after being placed in orbit.

In addition to the above description, the reference to the launch of the KH-11 is located within the *NASA Historical Data Book*, Volume VII, by Judy A. Rumerman. In chapter III, a brief mention is within the mission summary entries for STS-36. It states:

NASA Payload Deployed: None Other Government Payload Deployed: MS: David C. Hilmers, DOD KH 11-10 (AFP 731)

Other than this reference to the KH-11, not much data is known about the payload. Even the more complete breakdown within the *NASA Historical Data Book* outlines the fact that STS-36 was a classified mission:

This classified DOD mission launched February 28, 1990, from Kennedy Space Center and landed March 4 at Edwards Air Force Base. Launch was postponed several times (and then postponed further because of bad weather) because of the illness of the mission commander, John Creighton. The mission was the first time since the Apollo 13 mission in 1970 that a human spaceflight mission had been postponed because of the illness of a crew member.

This flight flew at an inclination orbit of 62 degrees, the highest inclination flown by the Shuttle to date. See Table 3-58 for further mission details.

If you noticed, NASA's website description of the payload makes reference to the KH-11 as a variant labeled as the KH 11-10. It also notes that the payload was "heavier" than other KH-11 satellites, and this was due to an important realization, albeit more of a rumor than anything else. This variant of the KH-11 was known as the *Misty*. Although a derivative of the KH-11, the *Misty* was rumored to have been invisible to all radar, and more importantly, hard to detect visibly as it orbited the earth.

A second *Misty* satellite was rumored to have been launched from Vandenberg Air Force Base on May 22, 1999, on board a TITAN IVB rocket. Although the KH-11s and their variants had the new capability of being launched from the space shuttle, they could still be put into orbit by a multi-staged rocket, if no shuttle mission was available to piggyback.

Overall, the *Misty* satellites are highly classified and not much is known. In a report entitled, "Reconsidering the Rules for Space Security," authored by Nancy Gallagher and John D. Steinbruner of the American Academy of Arts and Sciences, they outline the secrecy around the *Misty* satellites along with the future of them:

> Little is known about the capabilities of the stealth satellites in the *Misty* program. The objective is to prevent adversaries from calculating when any US satellite is in position to observe their activities, but amateur astronomers have sometimes been able to observe and track the first two *Misty* satellites launched in 1990 and 1999. The program drew congressional attention in 2004 when it was learned that the projected cost for launching a third *Misty* satellite by the end of the decade had almost doubled from $5 billion to $9.5 billion. That effort was reportedly cancelled in 2007.

THE NATIONAL RECONNAISSANCE OFFICE (NRO)

Programs such as those outlined in this chapter are incredibly interesting for many factors. Not only does it prove that the missions often had classified aspects not disclosed to the public, but they could be run by agencies that the general public has no idea even exist. The NRO, which spearheaded many of these programs outlined here, operated more than thirty years before the agency was ever officially acknowledged.

The NRO was officially established on September 6, 1961. It would take more than a decade before the public began whispering about the rumors of such an agency, but nothing was truly known or revealed. In fact, a declassified, formerly "Secret" memorandum was circulated within the NRO about the first rumors regarding the agency. A committee was established to study the security of the NRO, and the group had requested a breakdown of security breaches within the public that may have revealed the agency's identity. Only ten copies of the memorandum were created, and they were handed to those only with a strict need to know.

Although still heavily redacted, the memorandum dated January 7, 1974, written by the Chief, Special Security Center (name redacted) to the Chairman, Ad Hoc Group Studying Security of the NRO (name redacted), outlines eight breaches that revealed the identity of the NRO to the public:

The first mention of the NRO to appear in the public domain was in the *New York Times* of 22 January 1971 in the fifth of a series of articles by Benjamin Welles exploring the Nixon Administration's style in foreign policy. The article was titled "Foreign Policy: Disquiet Over Intelligence Setup." In a long article, Welles credits the NRO as part of the Defense Intelligence Agency. The exact wording on the NRO is: "Its (DIA) National Reconnaissance Office spends another 1 billion dollars yearly flying reconnaissance airplanes and lofting or exploiting the satellites that constantly circle the earth and photograph enemy terrain with incredible accuracy from 130 miles up."

The second reference to the NRO was made by Victor Marchetti in a series of radio and TV appearances during the period 21 September 1971 to April 1972. Marchetti refers to the National Reconnaissance Organization and correctly associates it as "this is the group that's in charge of the satellites, the spies in the skies."

The third use of material referring to the National Reconnaissance Office appeared in the *Christian Science Monitor*, 23 April 1973 in an article titled: "New Broom at CIA" by Benjamin Welles. In this article Welles discusses activities of Mr. James Schlesinger as head of the CIA. With reference to the "Intelligence Community Staff" Mr. Welles says: "On Schlesinger's order the ICS will comprise about 60—half CIA and the rest representing agencies involved in military intelligence—DIA, the code cracking National Security Agency, the National Reconnaissance Office, the State Department intelligence arm."

Fourth mention of the NRO was made in the *Chicago Tribune*, 27 April 1973, which carried a rewrite of the 23 April article by Welles in the *Christian Science Monitor*.

The fifth mention of the NRO occurred in the Congressional Record of October 12, 1973, when the National Reconnaissance Office was mentioned along with CIA, DIA and NSA.

The sixth reference to the NRO occurred in the Congressional Quarterly Weekly Report which reported on the activities of the Special Senate Committee to Study Questions Related to Secret and Confidential Government Documents. This Committee's report was the item in the Congressional Record of 12 October 1973.

The seventh mention in the press of the NRO was the Laurence Stern article in the Sunday, December 9, 1973, *Washington Post* titled: "$1.5 Billion Secret in the Sky. US Spy Unit Surfaces by Accident."

This was replayed in large measure in the *Olympian* Olympia, Washington on December 12, 1973. The article was titled "Its Initials are NRO . . . Very Hush-Hush." This then is the eighth article in the press which has come to our attention.

Despite the eight instances where the NRO's existence was leaked to the public, the NRO kept quiet and the US government never acknowledged it existed until September 18, 1992, when the Deputy Secretary of Defense announced it. The decision to finally officially acknowledge an agency that had operated for more than thirty years was based on a report by the CIA. The report was created in April of 1992, formerly classified "Secret," and recommended that the NRO's existence be declassified.

The report was entitled, "Report to the Director of Central Intelligence, DCI Task Force on The National Reconnaissance Office, Final Report." Within the cover letter that accompanies the final report, Robert Fuhrman, Chairman of the DCI Task Force on the NRO, wrote the following to the Deputy Secretary of Defense:

Our key recommendations for the Secretary of Defense, the Director of Central Intelligence and the Director of the NRO (DNRO) include the following:

- Retain the NRO as the single US government organization for development, procurement, and operation of overhead intelligence collection systems.
- Organize the NRO along functional ("INT") lines.

- Collocate the NRO in the Washington area by the end of 1993.
- Affirm a proactive role for the Intelligence Community in responding to operational as well as national needs. Adopt a new NRO mission statement reflecting this role.
- Combine the three budget Programs currently managed by the DNRO into a single integrated Overhead Reconnaissance Program.
- Strengthen the Intelligence Community's requirements process for system acquisition and for tasking.
- Declassify the "fact of" the NRO.
- Review the classification guidelines for NRO system characteristics and related intelligence products to improve the flow of information to those who need it.
- Encourage operational users and the Intelligence Community to employ actual overhead system in realistic exercises.
- Strengthen the National Reconnaissance Review Board and include operational issues in its mandate.

Figure 10.5. Although the NRO operated for decades when the public did not even know it existed, today it has a web page complete with job listings, details on the agency, and declassified information from the agency's "unacknowledged" years. *Credit*: **National Reconnaissance Office (NRO)**

Based on these recommendations, the world finally learned about the NRO and its mission. In today's world, the NRO plays a crucial role in keeping America safe. Its annual budget is entirely classified, and no one knows how much the agency spends on programs, research and development, or basic operational costs.

Unlike the days of old where the agency was just a rumor, today, it has a website, an online mission statement, and reams of information you can download about past programs. To the public in the twenty-first century, this is how the NRO describes itself:

When the United States needs eyes and ears in critical places where no human can reach—be it over the most rugged terrain or through the most hostile territory—it turns to the National Reconnaissance Office (NRO). The NRO is the US Government agency in charge of designing, building, launching, and maintaining America's intelligence satellites. Whether creating the latest innovations in satellite technology, contracting with the most cost-efficient industrial supplier, conducting rigorous launch schedules, or providing the highest-quality products to our customers, we never lose focus on who we are working to protect: our Nation and its citizens.

From our inception in 1961 to our declassification to the public in 1992, we have worked tirelessly to provide the best reconnaissance support possible to the Intelligence Community (IC) and Department of Defense (DoD). We are unwavering in our dedication to fulfilling our vision: Supra Et Ultra: Above and Beyond.

To me, the saga behind the NRO is toward the top of the list of America's best kept secrets. An agency that was responsible for designing an unknown number of spy satellites, implementing their strategy to make them work for American intelligence, and orchestrating the launch and integration of an untold number of these eyes in the sky operated for more than three decades. During that time frame, the public had little to no idea that the NRO even existed.

It also forces us all to think twice on whether we know what is truly going on within the secret world of the US government. When we think we understand a space shuttle mission, or the capabilities of a satellite, or whatever else we are told, more times than not, we are probably wrong. Secret agendas have existed for decades, and it usually takes decades for the secrets to be revealed.

THE PARANORMAL

11

THE UFO
PHENOMENON

One of the greatest questions that science has yet to answer is, "Are we alone in the universe?" For centuries, scientists have been asking that question and struggling to answer it. Because if it is determined life exists, somewhere, out in the cosmos—one must wonder can they, or are they, coming to Earth?

Although it is the story largely found in science fiction, extraterrestrial life visiting Earth would have enormous implications and possibilities for all of humanity. Naturally, regardless of no one being able to truly answer the question about being alone in the universe, there have been numerous witnesses to strange and unexplained phenomenon in the skies. This fuels the controversy, deepens the questions, and strengthens the case that quite possibly we are being visited by a race from another planet. But are we?

Oddly, there are thousands of records within the US government and military's files detailing Unidentified Flying Object (UFO) encounters that defy explanation. Just the mere existence of many of these documents goes against the official stance of the US government on the issue. As one would expect, that official stance includes a blanket denial that (1) UFOs are connected to extraterrestrials and (2) they pose any type of threat. That may sound reasonable, but when you look at the evidence, another story begins to emerge.

ROSWELL STARTS IT ALL

To best understand the US government and military's connection to the UFO story, you need to start from the beginning of it all. Arguably, what started the entire conspiracy and cover-up story was the "Roswell Incident."

Although the chronology of events slightly differs depending on the witness or researcher you talk to, the gist of the story goes like this: On or around June 14, 1947, farmer William "Mack" Brazel and his son discovered a UFO had crashed on their farm just outside of Roswell, New Mexico. On July 4, Brazel packed up his car with some of the debris that he found, and on July 7, drove it into town and delivered it to Sheriff George Wilcox.

The sheriff was just as confused as Brazel, so he contacted the military. Beginning with Colonel "Butch" Blanchard, who then passed word to General Roger Ramey, the military was perplexed as to what the debris was from, and how it got on Brazel's farm.

Major Jesse Marcel was tasked to go to the farm and collect the debris from the "crash site" on Brazel's ranch. On July 8, a statement to the press was made, and the "flying saucer" story was born.

Throughout the proceeding decades, the Roswell story would only get more convoluted, confusing, and ultimately even more unsolved. Many witnesses surfaced that talked about tales of bodies being seen at the Roswell Army Air Field (RAAF) hospital; wreckage that was seen by Jesse Marcel Jr., as shown to him by his dad; allegations that Major Marcel was forced to pose with wreckage that was not from the actual Roswell crash; and so many more claims that were near impossible to authenticate beyond any shadow of doubt.

The "Roswell Incident" became a legend. True or not, it will continue to be the capstone of a cover-up allegation that has only deepened in the twenty-first century. Since the events surrounding the Roswell incident have unfolded, the US government and military have offered multiple explanations over the past seven decades to explain the legend of what really happened at Roswell. The first real investigation into the Roswell incident was published by the General Accounting Office (GAO) in 1994. One of the biggest claims in this report, which is often overlooked by the general public, is the following statement:

In our search for records concerning the Roswell crash, we learned that some government records covering RAAF activities had been destroyed and others had not. For example, RAAF administrative records (from Mar. 1945 through Dec. 1949) and RAAF outgoing messages (from Oct. 1946 through Dec. 1949) were destroyed. The document disposition form does not indicate what organization or person destroyed the records and when or under what authority the records were destroyed.

This fact alone would make any researcher of any topic cringe. Evidence destruction will hinder any true investigation, so if records were shredded, how could you properly try to solve the case? That did not stop the US government from making the claim, because again, the above is often overlooked.

The explanations continued long after this GAO report. The US Air Force published *The Roswell Report: Fact Versus Fiction in the New Mexico Desert* in 1995, along with *The Roswell Report: Case Closed* in 1997. The latter has been the last, and supposedly final, explanation for the Roswell incident.

The *Roswell Report: Case Closed* offered the following bullet points:

- "Aliens" observed in the New Mexico desert were actually anthropomorphic test dummies that were carried aloft by US Air Force high-altitude balloons for scientific research.
- The "unusual" military activities in the New Mexico desert were high-altitude research balloon launch and recovery operations. Reports of military units that always seemed to arrive shortly after the crash of a flying saucer to retrieve the saucer and "crew" were actually accurate descriptions of Air Force personnel engaged in anthropomorphic dummy recovery operations.

The above seems plausible, right? Let's dig a little deeper to challenge it.

These crash test dummies were part of Operation High Dive, a secret project carried out by the US Air Force, which tested parachutes dropped from high altitudes. According to the air force, it was these dummies that could partially explain the multiple witnesses and their descriptions of "alien bodies" being seen at the RAAF. Except, there is one big problem with the story. A documented, historically proven, fact gets in the way that allows this to be true.

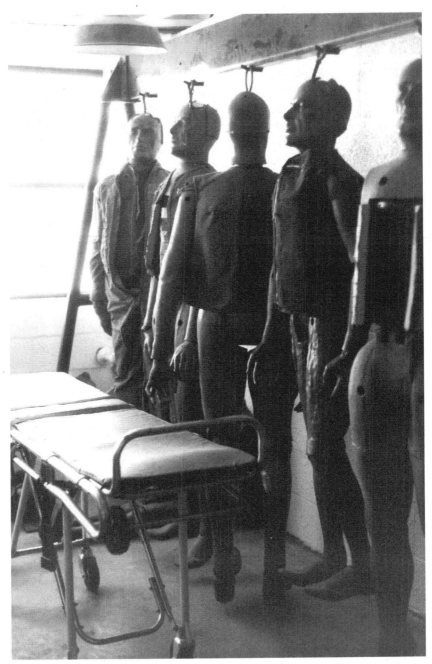

Figure 11.1. Official declassified US Air Force photograph of the crash test dummies. *Credit*: US Air Force

The very first crash test dummy invented was "Sierra Sam," created by Alderson Research Labs (ARL) and Sierra Engineering Company. The year of creation: 1949. It may take you a moment to realize, but there is a huge error here in history. Roswell occurred in 1947, approximately two years before the first crash test dummy was ever invented. Unless we just discovered time-traveling crash test dummies, how could the air force pass off such a theory to explain the alien bodies?

The lie goes deeper and gets much worse. The explanations continued in *The Roswell Report: Case Closed*:

- Claims of "alien bodies" at the Roswell Army Air Field hospital were most likely a combination of two separate incidents:
  - a 1956 KC-97 aircraft accident in which eleven air force members lost their lives; and
  - a 1959 manned balloon mishap in which two air force pilots were injured.

You can probably more easily see the blaring error with this one. Instead of a two-year time travel between the crash test dummies being invented and the year the Roswell incident happened, now the air force is passing off two other incidents to further explain the claims of "alien bodies."

Respectively, these incidents occurred nine and twelve years after the Roswell incident, and somehow, the military feels this is all okay to try and pass off to the public. I mean, we shouldn't let facts get in the way of a good story.

And the witnesses that corroborated all the above claims about alien bodies and wreckage? They all must have had their dates wrong, according to the US military. All of them.

The explanations are ludicrous. To get to the conclusion the US government and military has reached, you need to ignore the fact that there was destroyed evidence (why was it destroyed in the first place?); accept that hundreds of witnesses were mistaken and dates and memories recollected; and believe that crash test dummies could time travel. That is a tough pill to swallow for critical thinkers, but it is what the US government and military wants you to believe.

THE "COMPANY LINE"

Though the mystery about Roswell will linger for decades to come, it plays a crucial role in what I call the "Company Line." The "Company Line" is what I refer to as the official stance of the US government and military about UFOs. In fact, it is the first of two parts for the "Company Line." The other aspect is the US military's claim of investigating UFOs. Spoiler alert: their determination was that there is nothing to support UFOs are real, connected to extraterrestrials, or a threat to national security.

Fact Sheet

United States Air Force
Secretary of the Air Force, Office of Public Affairs, Washington, D.C. 20330

INFORMATION OF UFOs

Thank you for your request for information on the Air Force's investigation of unidentified flying objects, or UFO's.

The Air Force investigation of UFO's began in 1948 and was known as Project Sign. Later the name was changed to Project Grudge, and in 1953, it became Project Blue Book. Between 1948 and 1969 we investigated 12,618 reported sightings.

Of these sightings, 11,917 were found to have been caused by material objects (such as balloons, satellites, and aircraft), immaterial objects (such as lightning, reflections, and other natural phenomena), astronomical objects (such as stars, planets, the sun, and the moon), weather conditions, and hoaxes. As indicated, only 701 reported sightings remain unexplained.

On December 17, 1969, the Secretary of the Air Force announced the termination of Project Blue Book. The decision to discontinue UFO investigations was based on an evaluation of a report prepared by the University of Colorado entitled, "Scientific Study of Unidentified Flying Objects;" a review of the University of Colorado's report by the National Academy of Sciences; past UFO studies; and the Air Force's two decades of experience investigating UFO reports.

As a result of these investigations, studies, and experience, the conclusions of Project Blue Book were: (1) no UFO reported, investigated, and evaluated by the Air Force has ever given any indication of threat to our national security; (2) there has been no evidence submitted to or discovered by the Air Force that sightings categorized as "unidentified" represent technological developments or principles beyond the range of present day scientific knowledge; and (3) there has been no evidence indicating that sightings categorized as "unidentified" are extraterrestrial vehicles.

With the termination of Project Blue Book, the Air Force regulation establishing and controlling the program for investigating and analyzing UFOs was rescinded. All documentation regarding the former Blue Book investigation was permanently transferred to the Modern Military Branch, National Archives and Record Service, 8th and Pennsylvania Avenue, Washington DC 20408, and is available for public review and analysis.

Figure 11.2. US Air Force "fact sheet" on UFOs. *Credit*: US Air Force

To best explain the investigation, which lasted from 1947 through 1969, the US military created a "UFO Fact Sheet" that is often distributed by military branches and government agencies to offer a condensed explanation for what the UFO phenomenon is, and what it is not.

This "fact sheet" described "Project Blue Book," which was the most popular name out of a trifecta of projects aimed to tackle the UFO topic by the US military. It began with Project Sign in 1947, followed by Project Grudge in February of 1949, and then the effort became known as Project Blue Book in 1952. This lasted until the end of 1969 and was ultimately closed in January of 1970, simply because they felt they solved the mystery.

From 1947 to 1969, the Air Force investigated Unidentified Flying Objects under Project Blue Book. The project, headquartered at Wright-Patterson Air Force Base, Ohio, was terminated Dec. 17, 1969. Of a total of 12,618 sightings reported to Project Blue Book, 701 remained "unidentified."

The decision to discontinue UFO investigations was based on an evaluation of a report prepared by the University of Colorado entitled, "Scientific Study of Unidentified Flying Objects"; a review of the University of Colorado's report by the National Academy of Sciences; previous UFO studies and Air Force experience investigating UFO reports during the 1940s, '50s and '60s.

As a result of these investigations, studies and experience gained from investigating UFO reports since 1948, the conclusions of Project Blue Book were: (1) no UFO reported, investigated and evaluated by the Air Force was ever an indication of threat to our national security; (2) there was no evidence submitted to or discovered by the Air Force that sightings categorized as "unidentified" represented technological developments or principles beyond the range of modern scientific knowledge; and (3) there was no evidence indicating that sightings categorized as "unidentified" were extraterrestrial vehicles.

With the termination of Project Blue Book, the Air Force regulation establishing and controlling the program for investigating and analyzing UFOs was rescinded. Documentation regarding the former Blue Book investigation was permanently transferred to the Modern Military Branch, National Archives and Records Service, Eighth Street and Pennsylvania Avenue, N.W., Washington, D.C. 20408, and is available for public review and analysis.

Since the termination of Project Blue Book, nothing has occurred that would support a resumption of UFO investigations by the Air Force. Given the current environment of steadily decreasing defense budgets, it is unlikely the Air Force would become involved in such a costly project in the foreseeable future.

In short, the US government and military denies UFOs are real, denies they are a threat, and denies they warrant further investigation. Shocked? Yeah, me neither. However, this "fact sheet" offers the second part of the "Company Line." And this is exactly what *they* want you to believe about the UFO topic. They want you to just move along, and not ask any questions.

But what if you do? What if you challenge the "Company Line" and start digging deep into facts, figures, and official documents? This topic is what got this author interested in using the Freedom of Information Act (FOIA) in the first place. I was fifteen years old, fascinated by the UFO phenomenon, and I made a horrible mistake of thinking that if anyone would tell me the truth behind it all, it would be the US government!

Now now, be nice. I was fifteen years old, and even though I laugh at reminiscing that I considered such a thing, I sure am glad I thought it. Because it forced me to learn the FOIA, utilize it, attempt to master it (I don't think you really can), and employ it to its fullest potential. And in the end, it's the FOIA, along with the evidence it yields, that is the only thing you need to destroy the "Company Line," and prove there really is something to the UFO phenomenon.

THE NATIONAL SECURITY THREAT

There is a big argument within UFO circles on whether these "UFOs" actually pose a "threat" to humanity. It is highly debated, since many of those who are already in the "believer" category that aliens are visiting Earth, believe they would come here to destroy us. Although I am not in the full-fledged "believer" category, I do believe whatever the UFO phenomenon is, it could pose a severe threat on many levels.

The debate on hostile extraterrestrials is a different book in itself, but documentation does solidify there is a national security threat aspect to UFOs. In addition to that threat, many documents from decades ago not only defy explanation, but exhibit technology that still has yet to be adequately explained by any earthly means.

One of the earliest displays of this threat began back in 1952 when multiple UFOs appeared over some of the most sensitive airspaces within the borders of the United States. From July 12 to July 29, 1952, a large "UFO wave" of sightings was seen throughout the Washington, D.C., area. In fact, in 1952, Project Blue Book saw one of the biggest influxes of case reports they had ever seen. This enormous increase would remain the highest number all the way through to the end of their official investigation in 1969. No other year had as high of a number as 1952.

Some of these encounters were chronicled by the official historian of the CIA and the National Reconnaissance Office (NRO), Gerald K. Haines. He wrote in his publication *CIA's Role in the Study of UFOs, 1947–90—A Die-Hard Issue* the following:

> A massive buildup of sightings over the United States in 1952, especially in July, alarmed the Truman administration. On 19 and 20 July, radar scopes at Washington National Airport and Andrews Air Force Base tracked mysterious

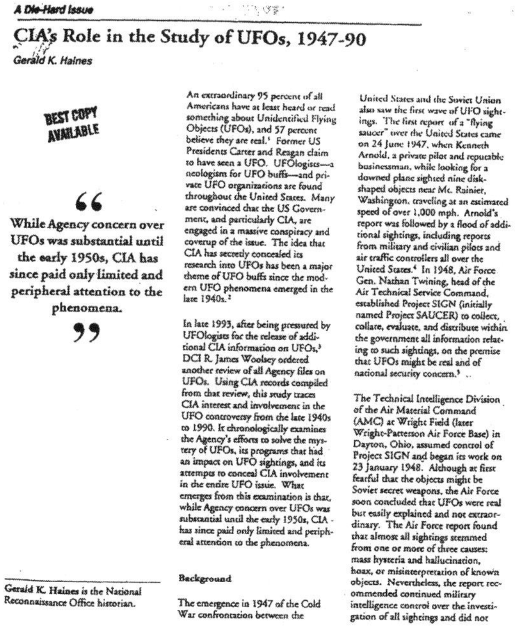

A Die-Hard Issue

CIA's Role in the Study of UFOs, 1947-90

Gerald K. Haines

BEST COPY AVAILABLE

"While Agency concern over UFOs was substantial until the early 1950s, CIA has since paid only limited and peripheral attention to the phenomena."

An extraordinary 95 percent of all Americans have at least heard or read something about Unidentified Flying Objects (UFOs), and 57 percent believe they are real.[1] Former US Presidents Carter and Reagan claim to have seen a UFO. UFOlogists—a neologism for UFO buffs—and private UFO organizations are found throughout the United States. Many are convinced that the US Government, and particularly CIA, are engaged in a massive conspiracy and coverup of the issue. The idea that CIA has secretly concealed its research into UFOs has been a major theme of UFO buffs since the modern UFO phenomena emerged in the late 1940s.[2]

In late 1993, after being pressured by UFOlogists for the release of additional CIA information on UFOs,[3] DCI R. James Woolsey ordered another review of all Agency files on UFOs. Using CIA records compiled from that review, this study traces CIA interest and involvement in the UFO controversy from the late 1940s to 1990. It chronologically examines the Agency's efforts to solve the mystery of UFOs, its programs that had an impact on UFO sightings, and its attempts to conceal CIA involvement in the entire UFO issue. What emerges from this examination is that, while Agency concern over UFOs was substantial until the early 1950s, CIA has since paid only limited and peripheral attention to the phenomena.

Background

The emergence in 1947 of the Cold War confrontation between the United States and the Soviet Union also saw the first wave of UFO sightings. The first report of a "flying saucer" over the United States came on 24 June 1947, when Kenneth Arnold, a private pilot and reputable businessman, while looking for a downed plane sighted nine disk-shaped objects near Mt. Rainier, Washington, traveling at an estimated speed of over 1,000 mph. Arnold's report was followed by a flood of additional sightings, including reports from military and civilian pilots and air traffic controllers all over the United States.[4] In 1948, Air Force Gen. Nathan Twining, head of the Air Technical Service Command, established Project SIGN (initially named Project SAUCER) to collect, collate, evaluate, and distribute within the government all information relating to such sightings, on the premise that UFOs might be real and of national security concern.[5]

The Technical Intelligence Division of the Air Material Command (AMC) at Wright Field (later Wright-Patterson Air Force Base) in Dayton, Ohio, assumed control of Project SIGN and began its work on 23 January 1948. Although at first fearful that the objects might be Soviet secret weapons, the Air Force soon concluded that UFOs were real but easily explained and not extraordinary. The Air Force report found that almost all sightings stemmed from one or more of three causes: mass hysteria and hallucination, hoax, or misinterpretation of known objects. Nevertheless, the report recommended continued military intelligence control over the investigation of all sightings and did not

Gerald K. Haines is the National Reconnaissance Office historian.

RELEASED July 1999

67

Figure 11.3. The cover page for the CIA's *CIA's Role in the Study of UFOs, 1947–90—A Die-Hard Issue* by Gerald Haines. *Credit*: Central Intelligence Agency (CIA)

blips. On 27 July, the blips reappeared. The Air Force scrambled interceptor aircraft to investigate, but they found nothing. The incidents, however, caused headlines across the country. The White House wanted to know what was happening, and the Air Force quickly offered the explanation that the radar blips might be the result of "temperature inversions." Later, a Civil Aeronautics Administration investigation confirmed that such radar blips were quite common and were caused by temperature inversions.

This excerpt is yet another prime example of what the US government and military does when giving explanations for UFO events. A plausible, well-worded explanation is given. To someone who would not care to dig deeper, it may even be accepted as documented fact, and not challenged by the everyday researcher touching on the UFO topic. But, what Mr. Haines fails to say is that the Project Blue Book files also had numerous sightings throughout the nation by human observers (and not just on radar), which confirmed structured craft of some kind that were flying above them, many of which were traveling at great rates of speed.

The absence of this detail by this government report shows that not all evidence is being offered to the public. In other words, the report implied that only radar sightings existed at this time, but, the actual case reports from their own Project Blue Book files involving witnesses of a human nature prove otherwise.

What the US government also fails to mention is members of their own military have gone on the record to give their statements about the Project Blue Book era, and the ridiculous nature of the conclusion set forth. One military officer to speak out at the time was Major Donald Keyhoe, a Marine Corps aviator.

Major Keyhoe published the book *Flying Saucers Are Real* in 1950. Toward the end of July 1952, he appeared on an archived film reel, and his tone was much different from the US Air Force's official statements at the time:

> With all due respect to the Air Force, I believe some of them will prove to be of interplanetary origin. During a three-year investigation, I have found that many pilots have described objects of substance and high speed. One case, the pilots reported their plane was buffeted by an object that had passed them at 500 miles an hour. Obviously, this was a solid object, and I believe it was from outer space.

Major Keyhoe's opinion was based on years of research, writing various articles, and studying the information that was available at the time. How could an experienced naval aviator, trained as a pilot, see the UFO evidence and become so convinced that it proved an extraterrestrial connection?

Another person to come forward was Dr. J. Allen Hynek. Dr. Hynek was the official scientific consultant for Project Blue Book, and he was often seen in the media debunking UFO cases through the 1950s. With every case that would cross his desk, he would have some type of "earthly" explanation for it and would put it into the "solved" category.

Dr. Hynek labeled cases as being nothing more than "swamp gas" or the "Planet Venus," and he often used other fallback explanations for the cases they were receiving. Everything seemed to be progressing. UFO cases were being explained, and the scientific approach seemed to be working—that is, until a huge problem for the military began to emerge.

As a scientist evaluating the evidence, Dr. Hynek began to turn from being a debunker and skeptic into a full-fledged believer. The testimonies, the photographs, and the film reels he was analyzing began to convince him that not only were UFOs real, they were not being adequately explained. His fallback explanations were no longer cutting it, and the military's ability to explain almost everything began to fail.

One case that is believed to have turned Dr. Hynek into a believer was the 1964 UFO encounter in Socorro, New Mexico. The witness was a police officer by the name of Lonnie Zamora. The case is still considered an "unknown" and is described in great detail within the Project Blue Book files:

On April 24, 1964, a Socorro, New Mexico, policeman, Mr. Lonnie Zamora, reported sighting an object about a mile south of the town at approximately 5:45 p.m., in an unpopulated area full of hills and gullies and covered with sagebrush. Following is a summary of his report to Air Force investigators:

Mr. Zamora reported that while chasing a speeding car north on US 85, he heard a roar and saw flames in an area where a dynamite shack was known to be located. He abandoned chase of the auto and proceeded to where he believed an explosion had occurred. After traveling a little-used road and experiencing considerable difficulty in trying to drive his car up a gravel-covered hill, he said he observed what he thought was an overturned car standing on end. At this point he was about 800 ft. distant from the object and his car was at the crest of a hill with the object ahead of him in a gully. He reported that during this first glance he saw one or two figures in coveralls whom he assumed to be occupants of the object. This is the only time he saw these figures; he did not see them again. After radioing to Police Headquarters at Socorro that he was proceeding to investigate what he believed to be an auto accident, he drove to a point about 150 ft from the gully where the object rested and stopped the car to proceed on foot. He said the object was white, egg- or oval-shaped and apparently supported on girderlike legs. He said he heard a roar and saw smoke and flame coming from the bottom of the object. At this point, Mr. Zamora believed that the object was about to explode and he became frightened, turned, and ran to shield himself behind the police car, bumping his leg and losing his glasses on the way. He said that he crouched down, shielding his eyes with his arm while the noise stopped and he glanced up. He reported that the object had risen to a point about 15–20 feet above the ground and the flame and smoke had ceased. At this point, he reported, he noted a design on the object which he described as markings in red about 1 to 1½ ft in height, shaped like a crescent with a vertical arrow and horizontal line underneath. He stated that the object remained stationary for several seconds and then flew off in a southerly direction following the contour of the gully.

Within moments afterward, Sgt. Chavez of the New Mexico State Police arrived on the scene in response to Mr. Zamora's earlier radio call. He observed no object, but he reported that there were some slight depressions in the ground and apparently burned brush in the area where Mr. Zamora had reported seeing the object. The brush was cold to the touch. Sgt. Chavez reported the incident to local military authorities who conducted the initial investigation.

The Air Force sent investigators from their project office at Wright-Patterson AFB, Ohio. The investigation disclosed the following facts:

No other witnesses to the object reported by Mr. Zamora could be located.

There were no unidentified helicopters or aircraft in the area.

Observers at radar installations had observed no unusual or unidentified blips.

There was no unusual meteorological activity; no thunderstorms. The weather was windy but clear.

There was no evidence of markings of any sort in the area other than the shallow depressions at the location where Mr. Zamora reported sighting the object.

Laboratory analysis of soil samples disclosed no foreign material or radiation above normal for the surrounding area.

Laboratory analysis of the burned brush showed no chemicals which would indicate a type of propellant.

In 1972, Dr. Hynek wrote and published his book entitled *The UFO Experience: A Scientific Inquiry*, where he shed new light on the intentions of the US military's UFO research. He repeatedly referenced what he believed to be the biggest problem—and that was the air force belief that "it can't be; therefore, it isn't."

Dr. Hynek believed this theorem was the root of the military's expectation for him to debunk rather than truly research. And that is exactly what he did for many years, before the evidence became too convincing to him. To anyone with a scientific background (or to anyone that just wants to use some common sense), this will not give you a credible scientific method or valid conclusion. It appeared that Dr. Hynek was hinting in his book that the military just assumed from the start that UFOs weren't real—and they would do anything to prove it. Their minds were already made up about what the UFO phenomenon really was.

Even in the post–Project Blue Book era, that would be from 1969 through the current date, there is extensive, highly classified documents to discover. Let me reiterate, these records should not even exist, since the US government and military denied interest after the close of Project Blue Book in 1969. Yet, literally thousands of pages exist.

One of my personal favorites is an incident that unfolded in Tehran, Iran, back in 1976. It came to me in the form of a four-page document from the Defense Intelligence Agency (DIA).

The story, according to this official document, goes like this:

In 1976, in Tehran, Iran, an unidentified object was seen over the city by local residents. This sighting sparked at least four phone calls to the nearest Imperial Iranian Air Force command post, and the senior officer on duty attempted to convince the callers they were simply seeing stars. He did not have any aircraft airborne and he thought nothing of it.

After the fourth call, however, he became intrigued enough to go outside and see for himself. Sure enough, he witnessed the object, which was much larger and brighter than any star in the sky. He realized he needed to take action.

He scrambled an F-4 Phantom jet to engage this unknown object. While on approach, the pilot reached 24 nautical miles away (27.6 miles) when something bizarre happened. The pilot lost all instrumentation and communication.

As the pilot broke off pursuit of the UFO, he regained it all, so he assumed it was a plane malfunction, and returned to base. Ten minutes later, a second F-4 Phantom jet was scrambled to intercept.

Upon reaching the same distance as the first jet of 24 nautical miles, something bizarre happened yet again. This time, the pilot witnessed the UFO begin to move away from his aircraft, keeping a constant distance of 24 nautical miles. The object, according to this document, would move as fast or as slow as it needed to keep that distance of 24 nautical miles exact.

The document then mentions a second object, which suddenly appeared out of the first UFO that the pilot was attempting to intercept. This second object began to head straight toward the F-4 Phantom at a great rate of speed. To any military pilot, if an object comes off of an aircraft and quickly comes toward you, that's an aggressive maneuver and most likely a missile—so you have to act fast.

The F-4 pilot quickly armed his AIM-9 missile to fire back. As he is ready to fire in 3 . . . 2 . . . 1 . . . everything shuts down. His communications, his instrumentation, it all goes offline, and his attempt to fire fails.

At this point, he is simply a sitting duck for what he believes is an incoming missile. Yet, before impact, this second UFO makes a turn, loops around his aircraft, and returns to the original UFO for a perfect rejoin. This was clearly not a missile, but what was it?

This story gets even more bizarre. A third UFO now appears out of the original craft. The pilot observes this third UFO descend straight toward the ground also at a great rate of speed, but right before impact, the object simply hovers and casts a light approximately 1½ to 2 miles in diameter over the area.

The report mysteriously skips the part about what happened next. After the light was cast on the ground, did aliens come out? Was there an explosion? Did it fly away into the cosmos at light speed? We do not know.

The report changes topic and explains that the pilot regained communications and most of his controls and he began his return to the base. The pilot continued to have instrumentation problems along the way, and during his return back, sees a fourth UFO. When the pilot radioed this sighting to the tower, they reported again that no air traffic was in the area. So, whatever this fourth object was, it too was unknown and should not have been in that vicinity.

The following morning, the second F-4 crew was flown by helicopter to the location where they believed the UFO may have landed the night before. Although they saw nothing on the ground, they questioned residents in a nearby house about the events that had recently unfolded. The residents reported seeing bright lights and hearing some loud noises, but that was all they reported. The last line of the report read that soil samples were taken for radiation testing, and the results would be forwarded when available.

That was the final line to this four-page document. After many attempts, I tried to find follow-ups that showed the result of the radiation testing, or subsequent investigation, to what these craft encountered in Iran were. There was nothing.

The fact that there is nothing to find ultimately means there are two possibilities. First, it's possible there is something to find, but it was destroyed or just denied that it exists. The second is that the US government and/or military never followed up. They never investigated further, and there really is not anything to find.

Beyond determining why there are no follow-ups, the biggest point that should be pointed out about this document is the classification level: unclassified. Why is that important? Because being such an astounding story, the US military chose not to classify it. Yet, other records show primarily redacted pages, classified all the way through to "Top Secret," and are still heavily redacted, if released at all.

If you can read the "1976 Iran Incident" documents, think about those "Top Secret" documents! What is underneath all that black that the US government and military feel is a threat to national security if they tell you?

Eventually, I found a classified version of the same report on the "1976 Iran Incident." Within the NSA archives was another copy of an intelligence report regarding that same incident.

However, this document had a crossed-out "Secret" stamp on every page. Next to that was a crossed-out "Confidential" stamp, which then was followed by a "Declassify on" stamp. What this means is the progression of classification to this particular intelligence report over time. When it was written, it was considered "Secret," the next level down from the highest classification of "Top Secret." In time the document was downgraded to a "Confidential" level and then later declassified to the public in 1981.

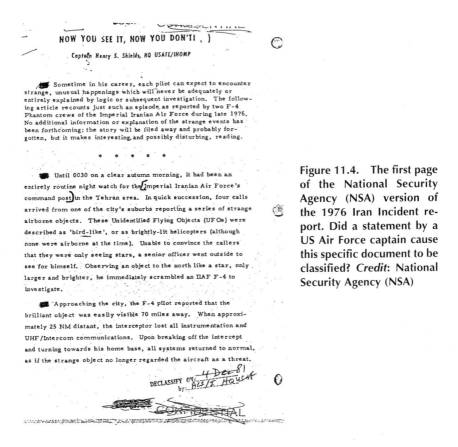

Figure 11.4. The first page of the National Security Agency (NSA) version of the 1976 Iran Incident report. Did a statement by a US Air Force captain cause this specific document to be classified? *Credit*: National Security Agency (NSA)

So why would the original report on the 1976 Iran Incident be "Unclassified" while this one was? The biggest difference that I could find in this previous "Secret" version was an introduction at the top written by a US Air Force pilot by the name of Captain Henry S. Shields. He stated:

Sometime in his career, each pilot can expect to encounter strange, unusual happenings which will never be adequately or entirely explained by logic or subsequent investigation. The following article recounts such an episode as reported by two F-4 Phantom crews of the Imperial Iranian Air Force during late 1976. No additional information or explanation of the strange events has been forthcoming; the story will be filed away and probably forgotten, but it makes interesting, and possibly disturbing, reading.

The remainder of the document, presumably written entirely by Captain Shields, outlined the 1976 Iran Incident. On many occasions within the record, he copied verbatim the details from the original DIA report. So could his introduction, where he stated that the report would be "filed away and probably forgotten" have motivated a "Secret" classification stamp? The mere fact that this US Air Force captain went on the record with such a strong statement, having come from the same agency that concluded UFOs were not a threat to national security, is a big deal.

This specific case also shows that whatever UFOs are, they can absolutely pose a threat. And Captain Shields goes on the record stating he believed it was all going to be filed away and forgotten. For decades, he was right.

THE REASON FOR SECRECY

One aspect to the FOIA that is not often used is the process of judicial review. If a researcher files a FOIA request and does not agree with the response (whether it be a denial or excessive redactions or various other reasons), the researcher can appeal the decision. Once the appeal is denied, even partially, the requester can take the agency to court for a judicial review.

Regarding UFOs, this happened back in about 1979, and the case offers an interesting look into why one agency, namely the National Security Agency (NSA), denies access to their UFO records. The Citizens Against UFO Secrecy, or CAUS, asked the NSA for UFO documents under the FOIA but was denied access to them. In total, the NSA discovered there were 239 documents responsive to their request. Seventy-nine of those had originated from other agencies, so as mandated by the FOIA, these documents were forwarded to those other agencies for review and release.

This particular action of forwarding records to another agency is quite common when using the FOIA. For example, many intelligence reports or other documents originate from one agency but are forwarded to many others for their intelligence purposes. Thankfully, agencies do communicate to a point with each other, but during the course of a FOIA request, if one of these documents is found, but determined it was written by another agency, that other agency is what is called the "Office of Primary Responsibility," or OPR. No government agency can declassify information or documents that originated from other agencies. In this case, seventy-nine of the UFO records were forwarded out for review and possible release.

The remaining UFO records, originating from within the NSA, were also reviewed for release. Very few were sent to CAUS, and the remaining number of records remained classified and withheld.

The step of taking a government agency into a courtroom is a right afforded to anyone utilizing the FOIA. In short, the progression to this stage is first you file a FOIA request. If you disagree with the release (or lack of release) of information, you can then go to step number two, which is appeal that decision. If you are denied your appeal, the third and final step afforded to us all is that you can sue under the FOIA and make your case in front of the judge.

CAUS v. NSA is incredibly important because this case reveals, quite literally, the reason "why" the NSA withheld their UFO records. During this case, CAUS submitted to the judge their argument for the release of the NSA UFO-related documentation. In response, the NSA created two affidavits to explain the reasons why the UFO information was to be withheld from the public, as they would not budge on their decision to hold on to the information.

The affidavits were written by the Chief, Office of Policy for the NSA, Eugene F. Yeates. The first of the two was considered the "Unclassified" version. This version was released to CAUS and the public, and that was intended to adequately explain the reason for withholding the information. What was not in this unclassified version was any information that would put "national security" information at risk. In other words, it was a softened-down version of the real reasons, which they were not really going to tell the public.

The second affidavit was for the judge only. This document was classified "Top Secret" and was handed to the judge to explain, in national security–threatening detail, why the UFO information was not to be released. However, judges do not have appropriate clearances to just read any and all classified information. So, in order for them to do so, they are given what is called an "in camera" clearance. This will then allow them to read the "Top

Secret" material in the affidavit. This allows them to review the appropriate information to make an adequate and informed decision.

In the end, the judge sided with the NSA. After reviewing the "Top Secret" version of the affidavit, the judge agreed that the information should be withheld, and supported that the information stay locked up away from the curious minds of the general public.

In time, that affidavit was also requested under the FOIA. It was eventually released in the early 1990s, but the original version the NSA sent out spoke volumes about how sensitive the UFO-related documents really were.

Not much can be gleamed from a record that is primarily blacked out and redacted, but that fact alone told an amazing story. It showed that whatever these UFO records were, they were classified, and they would remain so at the "Top Secret" level.

The release of these affidavits explained that most of the withheld documents related to Communications Intelligence, or COMINT. COMINT primarily contains information that is derived from the interception of foreign communications. According to the original release of the "Top Secret" Yeates affidavit:

> One hundred and fifteen of these reports were produced by the signals intelligence organization [REDACTED][REDACTED]. These COMINT reports are provided to NSA [REDACTED][REDACTED].

This is then followed by an entire paragraph that is blacked out. In fact, the entire page is sparse with words that are readable, but you can determine that the majority of the UFO-related documents withheld were COMINT reports collected from unnamed countries or sources. To be fair, the actual sources of the information would be properly classified, and I really do not necessarily disagree with them withholding those sources. In intelligence terms, they call this "sources and methods." In other words, it is where they got the information from and how they received it.

Looking beyond that necessity of classifying that information, it is the pure fact they are collecting UFO intelligence at all that becomes incredibly important. Not only was it the fact they are collecting it in the first place, but what was even more interesting, was *when* they were collecting it. The "Top Secret" Yeates affidavit explains:

The remaining one hundred and fifty-six records being withheld are communication intelligence (COMINT) reports which were produced between 1958 and 1979.

This fact contradicts the entire "Company Line" yet again. In 1969, those COMINT reports and intelligence papers should have ceased to exist all together. Also recall this affidavit was written in 1980, so the fact that it is stated they go up to 1979 essentially means that they were actively collecting this UFO intelligence and they had never stopped at any time.

NSA COMINT REPORTS ARE RELEASED

It took years and multiple FOIA requests to get the NSA to consider the release of the classified COMINT reports referenced in the Yeates affidavit. I know I was not the only one requesting the information, but I was fighting hard for them to release it all. Finally, after years of requesting, the NSA began to review the COMINT records for release.

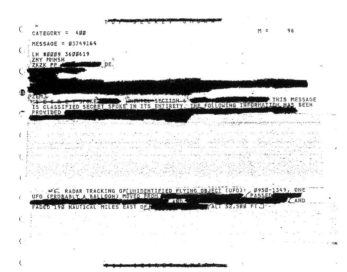

Figure 11.5. Single-page COMINT report clearly showing that the "Top Secret" information is still withheld from the public. *Credit*: National Security Agency (NSA)

I will admit I was quite excited to see that these records would finally be released. It was a huge fight and ultimately a triumph. I remember receiving the package for the first time and opening it up, because I knew that this would be it—a huge victory in the pursuit of the truth! At least, that was my thought as I was tearing open that package.

I realized the moment I pulled the records out of the envelope that there was a huge problem. Most of the records were fully redacted, and they were heavily blacked out and even whited out to lessen the striking visual appearance of "blacked-out" information. The documents were still considered classified as "Top Secret," which is why most of them were all redacted. In fact, some pages literally only had a few words that were readable; the rest was redacted or not released at all.

The fact that the documents were still classified "Top Secret" was a huge revelation on how sensitive these UFO documents remained. It also taught me that the NSA had not lost interest in the topic one bit.

These records do tell a story, despite the lack of detailed information. The fact they are dated well after 1969, the close of Project Blue Book, and the fact that are still considered "Top Secret" speaks volumes about how important they are.

So, what is beneath all those redactions?

WHEN IN DOUBT, LOSE THE DOCUMENTS

There is another way to officially request documents, which is used much less frequently than the FOIA, and that is called a Mandatory Declassification Review (MDR) request. An MDR is generally used for making an agency review, or re-review a record they may have previously released.

There are many differences here on a legal and overall technical nature, but an MDR is critical to getting information reviewed for release. During a FOIA request, let's say for "Project X," all documents are rounded up and reviewed for a release. In this example, I will say that the request was filed in the year 2000, and the requester received five hundred pages of material pertaining to their request, but many pages were blacked out.

Now let's say another researcher comes along in 2010 and submits an identical request for all files on "Project X." Generally, the agency can look back, see the information has been released in part before, and will send that batch of partially blacked-out records that were released in 2000. Case closed.

Can you catch what is wrong with that scenario? There is no second review, in most cases. The agency will continue to send out the same files as reviewed in 2000, for years and even a decade or decades beyond the original request. The issue I have with this is what is classified in 2000 is not necessarily classified in 2010. Therefore, you *should* conduct another review for the 2010 request, but sadly, agencies don't normally do that.

An MDR request can fix that for you. Instead of filing a FOIA request for the material, you can file an MDR and request that the responsive records are reviewed for possible release. I have done this many times before to get records re-reviewed, and am happy to say the process works. In many cases I was able to get the redacted portions re-reviewed, and when the documents were sent to me, I was happy to see that there was sometimes a lot less black on them.

That is the nutshell version of what the differences are, so I decided to fie MDR requests on the UFO-related material previously released by the NSA. These UFO records that the NSA have released, and those that have been withheld in full, have largely been sent out in the same manner for literally decades. The NSA will actually keep sending out the same documents that were originally blacked out in the 1980s and 1990s, to every requester who asks for them, but never conduct another review. That is, until it is requested in an MDR.

On July 24, 2013, I filed an MDR request to the NSA to have them look over all the previously released UFO records and see what, if any, blacked-out markings they could remove. It took nearly almost one full year to process, and on July 21, 2014, the NSA sent me a response.

They stated:

This responds to your request of 24 July 2013 to have previously released and redacted classified records pertaining to Unidentified Flying Objects (UFOs) currently posted on the Internet at URL http://www.nsa.gov/public info/declass/ufo/index.shtml reviewed for declassification. With the exception of the enclosed document, we cannot locate unredacted copies or the original documents that were previously reviewed and released to the public.

They lost them? *All* of them? How likely do you think that really is? Let's interpret this statement. When the NSA first reviewed these COMINT reports to be released, they did so in the mid to late 1990s, and reviewed the unredacted copies. They made a set of blacked-out/whited-out records to release, and somehow misplaced/shredded/lost all the originals.

That may not be surprising to some, with the track record of the US government's organizational skills, but from the viewpoint of someone who utilizes the FOIA, I would say that is not too common. Generally, these agencies will have multiple copies, in paper form and/or digital form, of every record they have in their original state. Yet, we are supposed to believe that the NSA somehow lost or destroyed some of the most sought-after UFO records to date.

THE IMPOSSIBLE IS TOUTED AS POSSIBLE

Despite overwhelming evidence of a national security threat, a continued UFO presence, and a present-day interest in the phenomenon, the US government and military alike tries to dismiss all possibility that UFOs are actually "unidentified." Back in 1997, the CIA published an article by the National Reconnaissance Office (NRO) historian Gerald K. Haines in the CIA's *Studies in Intelligence* internal newsletter. In this particular "Unclassified" article, Mr. Haines stated:

> In November 1954, CIA had entered into the world of high technology with its U-2 overhead reconnaissance project. Working with Lockheed's Advanced Development facility in Burbank, California, known as the Skunk Works, and Kelly Johnson, an eminent aeronautical engineer, the Agency by August 1955 was testing a high-altitude experimental aircraft—the U-2. It could fly at 60,000 feet; in the mid-1950s, most commercial airliners flew between 10,000 feet and 20,000 feet. Consequently, once the U-2 started test flights, commercial pilots and air traffic controllers began reporting a large increase in UFO sightings.
>
> The early U-2s were silver (they were later painted black) and reflected the rays from the sun, especially at sunrise and sunset. They often appeared as fiery objects to observers below. Air Force BLUE BOOK investigators aware of the secret U-2 flights tried to explain away such sightings by linking them

to natural phenomena such as ice crystals and temperature inversions. By checking with the Agency's U-2 Project Staff in Washington, BLUE BOOK investigators were able to attribute many UFO sightings to U-2 flights. They were careful, however, not to reveal the true cause of the sighting to the public.

In 2011, a declassified report originally designated "Secret" was released in part to the public. It was entitled, "The Central Intelligence Agency and Overhead Reconnaissance: The U-2 and OXCART Programs, 1954–1974." In this report, it also reinforced that the CIA was trying to "take credit" for the UFO sightings that spanned decades. They believed that the majority of them were actually U-2 flights, and although Project Blue Book officers knew the U-2 was to blame for many UFO-related events, they were part of the cover-up to that program's existence. At least, that's what the CIA wanted us to believe.

Finally, on July 2, 2014, a fairly controversial CIA tweet was posted on Twitter that showed the CIA was putting all their faith in this theory. The tweet read:

Remember reports of unusual activity in the skies in the '50s? That was us. #U2Week #UFODAY

The tweet then linked to the report I just mentioned.

That is a bold statement to make, don't you think? I mean, everything that happened in the 1950s was the CIA's U-2 program? It seems so straightforward, and written with such confidence, I would bet money that many people may believe such a statement, and then discount UFO reports all together. I would guess that was their intent, anyway.

That is, until you want to apply some logic and common sense. Let's only deal with the CIA documents to see if we can prove, or disprove, this outstanding tweet. First, let's go back to that case from 1957, wherein the document attempted to dismiss it away as a weather event, but logic tells us that a UFO was seen, crossing multiple states, jamming radars along the way and traveling at more than 2,300 mph and an elevation of 50,000 feet.

The U-2's top speed is 500 mph or Mach .67 (that's point 67). That is a far cry from taking credit for a 2,300-mph aircraft. Although the U-2 could fly at a reported 70,000 feet in the air, and that in itself matches the 50,000-

Figure 11.6. In the 1950s, the Central Intelligence Agency (CIA) tried to blame the U-2 as being the culprit for all UFO sightings throughout the decade. *Credit*: US Air Force / Master Sgt. Scott T. Sturkol / Released

foot altitude of the UFO, you would still not be anywhere near the speed to be the cause of it—therefore, we can easily dismiss that label.

In addition to juxtaposing this document to the U-2's capabilities, let's also know that the first flight of the U-2 was on August 1, 1955. That is more than halfway through the decade of the 1950s, yet the CIA claims their craft takes credit for everything. None of that makes any sense, because according to Project Blue Book statistics, there were at least 339 cases in the first half of the 1950s that were considered "unknown." Certainly, the CIA is not trying to rewrite history, or claim the U-2 also has time-travel capabilities?

The CIA has a long history on UFOs, but what deepens this mystery is their attempt to jump into the game in 2014 and try to essentially "take credit" for being the cause of the sightings. They then double-down on that claim, stating that the entire 1950s decade of UFO events was caused by their aircraft that only began flying in 1955.

Under the FOIA, I went after documents relating to this tweet. Yes, under the FOIA you can go after emails and internal memos that you may not think even exist, but when a CIA tweet is released, someone with access just does not make the lone decision to tweet it out. Tweets, and press releases, and whatever the CIA decides to disseminate to the public, has a decision-making process. In fact, there are social media strategy handbooks created by most agencies that outline what types of posts should, could, or should not appear under their respective social network accounts.

The CIA is no different, so I wanted to take a sneak peek and what their line of reasoning was for this statement. My request asked for the following:

1. All emails, memos, letters, correspondence etc. relating to the creation of this tweet. This would include, but not be limited to, the social network teams, web programmers, writers, and all CIA personnel involved in this tweet.
2. All documents compiled to research and fact-check for this tweet.

It took more a year to get a single page released by the CIA that pertained to the above. It gave an inside look at how much thought went into the tweet.

The single page was a succession of two emails, sent to and from unknown individuals, as the names are redacted due to a CIA statute protecting their identities. The first email was sent presumably to a boss or someone at a higher position with the agency that read:

I am almost afraid to bring it up, but it is apparently World UFO Day, who know (sic)?
  We could tie it into U2 Week!
  Reports of unusual activity in the sky in the '50s? That was just us. #U2Week #UFODay
  Link to the U-2 doc and photo of excerpt—attached.
  I use that line in my tours, it always goes over well.

The response from the recipient of the above was short and sweet. Whomever this email went to simply replied with the following:

I love it. Good to go

The response was so rushed, they forgot an end period on their email. The first email was so rushed, they didn't even use proper grammar. Although I tend to not judge and go into "Grammar Nazi" mode, it is indicative of the amount of thought that went into this blast to their followers. Not only was it inaccurate, it was downright misleading and lacked any thought or research.

Recall my specific request. I asked for all documents and emails that would show the fact-checking and entirely who was involved and at what levels research was even done. Go back and reference a few paragraphs and re-read what I asked for. You would think that such a bold statement by the CIA, and then my request, it would all yield more than a single page relating to what I requested. Yet, there was just this one single page of two emails. It clearly showed no thought, no research, and no fact-checking.

THE FUTURE OF UFO "DISCLOSURE"

When I wrote my first book, *Inside The Black Vault: The Government's UFO Secrets Revealed*, news had recently broke about a "Secret Pentagon UFO program" known as the "Advanced Aerospace Threat Identification Program," or AATIP. The notion behind it all is exciting. However, along with the reveal came much controversy about whether the program is really what the media, and others who claim to have worked on the program, claim that it is. Therefore, because official documents are incredibly scarce as of the writing of now both manuscripts, it is hard to accurately report on without speculating.

Despite the controversy and lack of information, there have been some positive developments in 2019 that may shed some light on future "disclosures" by the US government and military.

In April of 2019, Politico reported the US Navy was creating "UFO Reporting Guidelines" that would allow pilots an outlet to file an official report of any sightings of unknown objects. Through a FOIA request, I was able to obtain internal navy emails that described what these "guidelines" are.

One email, written by John F. Stratton, Senior Analyst, Nimitz Operational Intelligence Center, Office of Naval Intelligence, stated the following:

> Safety of aircrew is always a paramount concern to the US Navy and the Department of Defense. The wide proliferation and availability of inexpensive unmanned aerial systems (UAS) such as commercially available quadcopters has increasingly made airspace de-confliction an issue for our aviators. In this increasingly complex airspace including both military and civilian aviation environments, the US Navy is proactive in exercising due diligence in investigating any observation in training areas that could affect the safety of our aircrew. Based on this increased airspace complexity, US Navy aircrew were

provided with reporting instructions in order to determine the frequency and location of any UAS operating in our training areas.

In response to past reports, the US Navy issued guidelines for responses to observations. Based on continued reporting under those guidelines, the US Navy has decided to further develop ways to help better understand the source and nature of the observations. As an example, in 2012 there were a number of lasing events near Naval Air Station Oceana, the US Navy took these hazards to aviation very seriously and working with Law Enforcement identified and prosecuted the individual. While the US Navy acknowledges that these hazards to aviation may be inadvertent or unintended, just as with the lasing events, the US Navy remains vigilant in addressing any and all hazards to aviation.

We are currently updating guidelines to be more aircraft specific in order to facilitate reports that support an objective data driven analysis while helping to remove any stigmas from reporting anything unknown in the airspace. Due to the operational and aircraft specific nature of these guidelines, security considerations preclude their disclosure. The US Navy is at the forefront of this effort but works across the Department of Defense to ensure other service partners maintain awareness for the safety of their aircrew. The US Navy is not working with any entities outside of the US government.

Military and civilian aviation has always had channels for reporting airspace violations and hazards to aviation safety.

However, based on the enhanced guidelines that were implemented reporting became more consistent which lead to our recognition that more specific guidelines were needed. The US Navy continues to operate and train safely throughout the world.

This statement was then edited down to the public version and sent to Politico and other news outlets by Joseph Gradisher, spokesperson for the US Navy, and quoted in the media:

There have been a number of reports of unauthorized and/or unidentified aircraft entering various military-controlled ranges and designated air space in recent years. For safety and security concerns, the Navy and the USAF take these reports very seriously and investigate each and every report. As part of this effort, the Navy is updating and formalizing the process by which reports of any such suspected incursions can be made to the cognizant authorities. A new message to the fleet that will detail the steps for reporting is in draft. In response to requests for information from Congressional members and staff,

Navy officials have provided a series of briefings by senior Naval Intelligence officials as well as aviators who reported hazards to aviation safety.

Although there's not much mention of UFOs, other than "unidentified aircraft," it is encouraging to see that members of Congress were, and possibly continually are, being briefed about the topic.

In addition to the above, after a decade's long denial of interest in UFOs, the Pentagon admitted to the *New York Post* in May of 2019, through an official statement, that the AATIP program *did* investigate UFOs, or what they now call Unidentified Aerial Phenomena (UAPs).

This admission came from Mr. Christopher Sherwood, spokesperson, Department of Defense, and included the following, in part:

> The Department of Defense is always concerned about maintaining positive identification of all aircraft in our operating environment as well as identifying any foreign capability that may be a threat to the homeland. The department will continue to investigate, through normal procedures, reports of unidentified aircraft encountered by US military aviators in order to ensure defense of the homeland and protection against strategic surprise by our nation's adversaries.
>
> The AATIP program did pursue research and investigation into unidentified aerial phenomena.

There is much yet to be revealed about the AATIP program, those who claim involvement in it, UFOs, UAPs, and the future of possible "disclosures." Some may believe there is much to disclose by the US government, including the reality of extraterrestrials. Others may doubt there is anything to disclose, and it is all an embellished and overhyped myth.

Regardless of what the answer to that riddle is, and whether a disclosure of any kind will take place, there is a lot that evidence establishes. The UFO phenomenon is real. It exhibits technology that far surpasses technology of the day, even by decades. And some of the case details exhibit a clear threat to national security.

Only time will tell if this all will be adequately explained. But given the fact that more than seventy years have passed since the Roswell incident, and that has yet to happen, may indicate it never will.

12

THE CIA'S REMOTE VIEWING PROGRAM

The hunt for mind-control techniques was a dark era for the history of the Central Intelligence Agency (CIA), but it is extremely important to the overall understanding of the intelligence community. Despite the horrific outcome of the experiment that led to the death of Dr. Frank Olson, the aim of experiments like that showed there was much more to explore for intelligence-gathering purposes that involved "fringe" thinking and scientific methods that were not, shall we say, "textbook" approaches.

Beginning in the 1970s, more than twenty million dollars was allocated and spent over the span of approximately twenty years. This effort was to investigate what became known as "remote viewing," or the psychic ability to "see" remote places. This ability harnessed the power of the human mind and aimed to see if intelligence could be gathered, from half a world away, using only thought and clairvoyance.

On November 30, 1995, the *Los Angeles Times* published an article by R. Jeffrey Smith and Curt Suplee that outlined the scope of "remote viewing" programs:

> US military and intelligence officers spent as much as $20 million over two decades consulting psychics and others with suspected paranormal powers in an attempt to obtain—on the cheap and in a hurry—information pertinent to national security that was unavailable elsewhere.
>
> As recently as 1993, a military agency asked the psychics to help locate tunnels suspected of being dug by North Korea under a demilitarized zone

separating it from South Korea. Another federal agency sought to learn the precise jobs of individuals in various criminal organizations, while a third agency sought to learn the whereabouts of enemy spies.

In the beginning days of the research, the CIA created and funded a program that they ultimately called SCANATE. This is believed to be one of the earliest aspects of the "remote viewing" research by the intelligence community, which began in 1970. Some of the allocated research money by the CIA went to Stanford Research Institute (SRI) International, headquartered in Menlo Park, California. The program at SRI International was led by engineer Dr. Harold E. Puthoff and physicist Russell Targ, and they explored various aspects to "remote viewing" techniques and tested whether the research aim held any promise for becoming a viable intelligence-gathering method.

In a declassified "Secret" report from December of 1979, entitled, "The Grill Flame Scientific Evaluation Committee," the CIA's SCANATE program was described in depth:

This series of studies relates to long distance remote viewing by specification of geographical coordinates. Targets which were viewed in this fashion include a West Virginia site, a Urals site, Kerguelen Island, Project Atlas, the Sylvania Laser Laboratory in California, the Berkeley Laboratory Bevatron in California, Utah and China Lake sites, and several USSR sites.

Interestingly, the author of this document, Mr. Manfred Gale, who served as chairman of the scientific committee evaluating the program, expressed concerns over the validity of the tests:

In general, the Kerguelen Island and West Virginia site results appear impressive. That is, the sketches and detailed verbal statements appear to match characteristics of the targets quite well until one carefully considers the timing and the notion that each subject could have obtained the impressive detailed information during the day that ensued between the first and second "readings" of each target. Specifically, following submission of the first reading, each subject chose to "visit" again and obtain additional more detailed information. This more detailed information is that which appears to provide a great match to the target characteristics. Similarly, inconsistent and conflicting detailed reporting causes the careful reader to be at least slightly suspicious. In all fairness, these were early attempts in the research program and the investigators were just beginning to feel their way. More critical evaluation should be applied to the longer distance and subsequent targets.

In order to determine if the tests were indeed "suspicious," one must learn how they were conducted. Using double-blind methods, third-party panels to evaluate the results, and pure random selections were only a few of the characteristics of the tests conducted. Although there are tens of thousands of records that have been released about this program and the tests at SRI International, a third-party contractor was brought in to evaluate all of the information toward the end of the 1970s. Their goal was to ultimately formulate an opinion on whether the work conducted on "remote viewing" was beneficial to continue. That specific contract was 77F 104420 and awarded to Systemetrics, located in Blacksburg, Virginia.

The result was a near three-hundred-page study entitled, "Summary and Critical Evaluation of Research in Remote Viewing," published on June 1, 1979. This report began by offering in-depth details on how the "remote viewing" tests were conducted:

> In the training mode of this sequence, "100 targets on the earth's surface, ten per day for ten days, were chosen at random, often by different experimenters. For each ten-trial session, the experiment would begin with the subject ([Ingo] Swann) being given a target location by latitude and longitude only, for which he had to provide an immediate response of what he saw. Following his response, some brief indication was given as to whether there existed any correspondence between his description and the target location . . . A run of ten coordinates was always completed in less than thirty minutes for the entire run." (Project SCANATE Report, no date, pp. 1–2)
>
> The experimenters were impressed with the results. As indicated in Targ and Puthoff (1977, p. 28), "even though the descriptions were perhaps a bit vague here, a little ambiguous there, they were accurate enough to make us begin to wonder whether we had on our hands a case of paranormal remote viewing or paranormal memory." They recognized (SCANATE Report, p. 2) that the results were only indicative, since "even under the carefully controlled experimental conditions in force, a) an individual could, in principle, obtain good results on the basis of memory, and b) given the hypothesis of extra-ordinary functioning an individual could, in principle, obtain the data subliminally from an experimenter who knows the target location." They recognized at that time the need for "double-blind" targets in successive tests.

The review also offered some improvements for future testing of the viewers utilized in the program. However, Systemetrics noted that they may not have the capability to adequately fine-tune the research. They stated:

Lengthy, careful study would be required to develop a safe, perhaps foolproof protocol. Experience with this general type of research would be required to refine the protocol further, to render it acceptable to the behavioral science research community. Such is beyond our scope and responsibility in this report, and perhaps beyond our capability.

Despite being unable to adequately address all fine-tuning elements to the study, Systemetrics did outline some of the people involved with the study. As referenced in the previous excerpts, one person heavily immersed in the experiments was claimed psychic Ingo Swann. According to his online biography at his personal website:

INGO SWANN (September 14, 1933–January 31, 2013) was internationally known as an advocate and researcher of the exceptional powers of the human mind, and as a leading figure in governmental and scientific projects to investigate and identify the scope of subtle human perceptions.

The biography goes on to state:

Ingo's early work in parapsychology, as a noted and highly successful "guinea pig," made him a psychic superstar in that field. His subsequent research on behalf of American intelligence interests, including that of the CIA, won him top PSI-spy status.

It is unclear what "top PSI-spy status" truly means, or if that is a self-proclaimed title, however, Swann is mentioned many times throughout CIA records declassified on the project, and he was very active in the beginning stages of the SCANATE program. Swann was also heavily involved with SRI International in regards to studies on psychic research in psychokinesis. During this, Swann had told Puthoff and Targ that he could "look anywhere in the world" if they just gave him some coordinates like latitude and longitude.

It seems like at first, there was not much faith in the experiments. This sequence of events is referenced in the "Summary and Critical Evaluation of Research in Remote Viewing" report:

Ingo Swann, suggested that the experimentation could be made more interesting because he could "look anywhere in the world if you just gave me some coordinates like latitude and longitude." (Targ and Puthoff, 1977, p. 27)

Initial "experiments" were done largely to placate Swann; however, when these were considered to be successful, more controlled experiments and a "standard" protocol were developed. The remote viewing effort was enlarged, various subjects were used, near and far targets were selected, individual success predictors were evaluated, and several sponsors supported the work.

Swann was then further involved with tests that had him look at latitude and longitude coordinates to test what he could "see" about those locations. He was never told what the locations were; he was just given the coordinates. These locations included a site in the Soviet Union, a volcano in Iceland, the ocean, and Lake Eyre in Australia, among many others. The results displayed varying degrees of success but showed enough promise to continue the program and catch the attention of the intelligence community.

SRI International brought together a somewhat interesting group of "consultants" that offered their abilities to the research. Obviously, Ingo

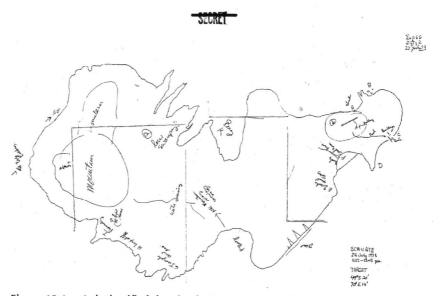

Figure 12.1.　A declassified drawing by Ingo Swann during one of the remote viewing sessions. *Credit*: Central Intelligence Agency (CIA)

Swann was a key player in many of the tests early on, but records reveal that so was Israeli-British illusionist, magician, and self-proclaimed psychic Uri Geller.

According to one document, written by SRI International, tests showed that Geller had a high degree of success. During the period of August 4–11, 1973, Geller took part in many experiments. The record, entitled, "EXPER-IMENTS—Uri Geller at SRI, August 4–11, 1973," details the objectives:

> The objective of this group of experimental sessions is to verify Geller's apparent paranormal perception under carefully controlled conditions and to head toward an understanding of the physical and psychological variables underlying his apparent ability.
>
> In each of the eight days of this experimental period we conducted picture drawing experiments. In these experiments Geller was separated from the target material either by an electrically isolated shielded room or by the isolation provided by having the targets drawn on the East Coast. We have continued to work with picture drawing tasks in an effort to achieve repeatability so that we could meaningfully vary the experimental conditions to determine the effect of physical parameters on the phenomena. As a result of Geller's success in this experimental period, we consider that he has demonstrated his paranormal perceptual ability in a convincing and unambiguous manner.

As outlined in the same document, for the test experiments on Saturday, August 4, Geller was shown two drawings. Here was the breakdown of his results:

> Two drawing experiments were conducted this day. In both of these, Geller was closeted in an opaque, acoustically and electrically shielded room. This room is the double-walled shielded room used for EEG-research in the Life Sciences Division of SRI. It is locked by means of an inner and outer door, each of which is secured with a refrigerator-type locking mechanism.
>
> The two drawings used in this experiment were selected by randomly opening a large college dictionary and selecting the first word which could reasonably be drawn. The first word obtained in this manner was "fuse" and the object drawn was a firecracker. All target selection and picture drawing was done with Geller already in the shielded room. Geller was notified via intercom when the target picture was drawn and taped to the wall outside his enclosure.

Figure 12.2. During the sessions, Uri Geller was locked in this room, as shown here with one of the assistants pictured. *Credit*: Central Intelligence Agency (CIA)

His almost immediate response that he saw a "cylinder with noise coming out of it." (He was continuously monitored by a one-way audio circuit.) His drawing to correspond to the target was a drum, along with a number of other cylindrical-looking objects.

The second word selected was "bunch," and the target was a bunch of grapes. Geller's immediate response that he saw "drops of water coming out of the picture." He then talked about "purple circles." Finally, he said that he was quite sure that he had the picture. His drawing was indeed a bunch of grapes. Both the target picture and Geller's rendition had 24 grapes in the bunch.

In this work the target picture is never discussed by the experimenters after the picture is drawn or brought near the shielded room. The intercom operates only from the inside of the room to the outside, except when the push-to-talk switch is depressed on the outside of the room. In our detailed examination of the shielded room and the protocol used in these experiments no sensory leakage has been found, nor has any defect in the protocol been brought to our attention.

For Geller to pinpoint not only the image, but the exact number of grapes, this would no doubt catch the attention of the intelligence community. What if this technique could be utilized, that could allow a viewer to pinpoint precise locations of troops, artillery, or land mines on the battlefield? What if from half a world away, a viewer could tell intelligence officers what types of weapons were being readied by America's enemies?

Although "remote viewers" could not always get an exact match, these types of successes like with Geller spawned more money and additional agencies to jump in and attempt to see if there was value to this sort of research. One such project that followed SCANATE was initiated by the US Army Intelligence & Security Command (INSCOM). Its aim was also to see what value there was to "remote viewing" research. This specific effort was known as Project Grill Flame, which began in fiscal year 1981. INSCOM also tapped SRI International to tackle some of the research goals, since they had already done work associated with the phenomenon.

In a declassified August 20, 1981, "Secret" document as released by the CIA, it described Project Grill Flame as the following:

> Project GRILL FLAME is an Army and DIA jointly financed effort to study novel intelligence collection techniques. The fiscal year 1982 justification material states that GRILL FLAME studies will help to identify the capabilities and vulnerabilities associated with paranormal phenomenon having military applications.
>
> GRILL FLAME is a planned three year joint program which is in its first year (FY81) between DIA and the Army to investigate in detail certain paranormal phenomenon, such as, remote viewing and psychokinesis that have potential military applications. Emphasis this year has been on evaluating application potential and limitations of remote viewing (the ability of individuals to mentally collect data at a distance) phenomena and to evaluate the significance of foreign work, particularly as it may pose a threat to the United States.

Let me just state for the record, the exact genesis and scope for all of these "remote viewing" projects is hard to follow. With many agencies involved, pulling from various funding mechanisms, it's hard to track exactly who was sharing information with who, if at all. Thousands of pages have been declassified and released to the public regarding these research projects, and they show various experiments and tests with varying degrees of success, but also, much overlap between contractors and consultants. This also makes it very difficult to make a cohesive story line of how it all unfolded.

I often wrestle between two schools of thought in regard to "remote viewing." The first is the reality that in many cases, the left hand does not know what the right hand is doing. In other words, there is no sharing of information, and in many instances throughout history, agencies will often fund the same type of research simultaneously. The end result is a mismanagement of funds, and research is often duplicated.

The second school of thought is whether this massive jambalaya of documents, reports, and committee evaluations is intended to create confusion for researchers such as myself. For document researchers, we see that time and time again. We will push and push for records to be released on a certain topic, they are, but in the tune of tens of thousands or even hundreds of thousands of pages (if not more). That then creates a long-standing hurdle to leap over, in regards to how long it will take to go through records, make a cohesive story line, and offer the public a better understanding of the subject at hand.

You will note that throughout this chapter there is a seemingly wide array of conclusions about whether "remote viewing" was a viable intelligence-gathering method. It's like when you read one report, there was no success at all with the experiments and the tests conducted were questioned on their scientific validity and method. Read another document, and Geller drew the precise number of grapes on a stem when asked to draw what he sees. Of all the things that could have been his target "picture" to conjure in his mind, that's pretty amazing to think about, if true.

Of course, it could all be a rather staggering coincidence, and he just "got lucky"—but documents reveal he had other "hits," as they were called, when viewing the images in his mind. So, which school of thought about this is right?

The answer to that is pretty much unclear, but these documents also reveal another motivator for some: money. Never a fun accusation to consider, but when talking about tens of millions of dollars at play, is it plausible that someone may skew a scientific result or two? Keep in mind what was already established earlier in this chapter that was written within one document evaluating the scientific method used in these experiments. In "The Grill Flame Scientific Evaluation Committee" document, the chairman stated, "inconsistent and conflicting detailed reporting causes the careful reader to be at least slightly suspicious."

I would never state that is what really happened during the "remote viewing" experiments, but it's always something to consider, given the fact that illusionists and magicians were involved. If you read my first book, *Inside The Black Vault: The Government's UFO Secrets Revealed*, you will know I am a huge fan of magic, and one can learn quite a bit from it. One of those things is fooling the audience into thinking something that is not necessarily true.

On this note, documents also reveal the frustration that some had that more money was not flowing their way for their paranormal abilities. One record, declassified from a "Secret" designation, outlines that Swann was also not involved in Project Grill Flame, but he grew quite upset that he himself did not receive additional funding from INSCOM for his niche of research and ability.

The memorandum, dated 12 December 1980, was written by Lieutenant Colonel Murray B. Watt, project manager for INSCOM's Grill Flame project, and he stated the following:

> During my meeting with Ingo Swann I learned that he (Swann) was upset that Army had apparently chosen not to back the development of his "new training program" and that Army was instead proposing to put their money into other aspects of the program. Apparently, Mr. Swann felt that his briefing to Army personnel in late July 80 had been given for the purpose of obtaining funds from Army. In a later meeting with [REDACTED] the subject came up again. I informed [REDACTED] that I had not perceived the July 1980 meeting as a "pitch" for funds, and at that time in response to our questions Mr. Swann had stated that his program would not be completed for almost 1 year at which time we could negotiate for having some of our personnel trained. At this time, Swann does not appear ready to agree to training any outsiders unless he has complete control over the selection process, and any follow-on training that might be needed. He reacted in a very hostile manner to my inquiry about the possibility of some people receiving training in the next year or so. Again [REDACTED] explained this hostile attitude as being a result of Swann's perceived idea that the Army did not want to back his program. [REDACTED]

went on to explain that even though DIA will be funding this aspect of the overall program there will not be enough money to see the training program through completion. In response to whether or not Army would be willing to put some dollars into this segment of the program, I told [REDACTED] I would let OACSI know of his concern and that he should bring the subject up at the quarterly Grill Flame meeting on the 23d of Jan 81.

When Grill Flame was canceled in fiscal year 1983, a report was written to summarize the findings. These types of reports are very useful, as it truly does summarize, in some cases, tens of thousands of pages accumulated over the course of many years and offers a baseline conclusion on how the project went. It also, in some cases, helps researchers determine whether or not the intelligence community determined it was successful.

In the October 19, 1983, "Grill Flame Project Report," declassified from a "Secret" status, it summarizes Grill Flame's findings:

> This report summarizes results of the three-year GRILL FLAME project, which terminated at the close of FY 1983. It contains key findings from the various project activities, and identifies potential follow-on efforts. The types of investigations, methods used for their evaluation, and other aspects of the GRILL FLAME project also are reviewed. Additional project information is summarized in the appendices, and detailed project reports are listed in the bibliography.

The document then sheds more light on the Grill Flame program:

> Project GRILL FLAME was a joint OIA and Army effort, with OIA provid-ing overall project management and coordination. The project's main goals were to evaluate the threat that foreign psychoenergetics achievements might pose to US national security, and to explore the potential of psychoenergetics for use in US intelligence collection.
>
> Psychoenergetics refers to classes of human capabilities that are para-psychological in nature. There are two main categories, informational and energetic, that can be defined as:
>
> 1. Remote viewing (RV)/Extrasensory Perception (ESP)—ability of an individ-ual to access and describe remote geographic areas or to access and describe concealed data via undefined transmission mechanisms.

2. Psychokinesis (PK)—mental ability to influence physical or biological systems via undefined physical mechanisms.

The primary focus of the GRILL FLAME effort was on remote viewing phenomena. However, psychokinesis research in the USSR, China and other foreign countries was examined to see if the occurrence of remote viewing could be detected by scientific instrumentation. This has implications for possible countermeasures to foreign use of remote viewing.

The report then went on to summarize the findings, and it offered an interesting conclusion:

Key findings of the GRILL FLAME project are:

- Remote viewing is a real phenomenon, and is not degraded by distance or shielding.
- Remote viewing ability can be improved by appropriate training procedures.
- Remote viewing has potential for US intelligence applications. However, at this stage of development, descriptive content (e.g., sketches, configurations) is more reliable than analytic content (e.g., function, complex technical data).
- A potential threat to US national security exists from foreign achievements in psychoenergetics. In the USSR and in China, this research is well funded and receives high-level government backing.

Achievements of the GRILL FLAME project include development of remote viewing training methods, the development of statistical methods for evaluating remote viewing data, and the compilation of an extensive database on foreign psychoenergetics research. Methods for improving the reliability of remote viewing data, through detailed understanding of the remote viewing process, and through identification of techniques for isolating valid from spurious data also were achieved. Training techniques that show promise for enhancing the reliability of the analytical content of remote viewing data also were identified.

After GRILL FLAME ended, the effort was transferred from the INSCOM over to the Defense Intelligence Agency (DIA), where it was renamed SUN STREAK. From the mid-1980s through approximately the next decade, there were as many as a hundred additional tests performed.

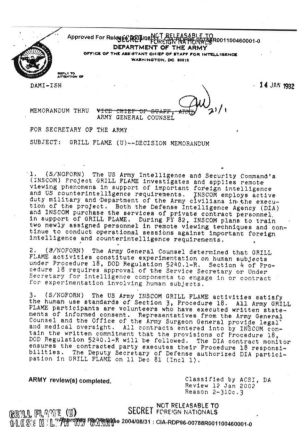

Figure 12.3. Just one of the tens of thousands of pages declassified from Grill Flame and other remote viewing programs. *Credit*: Central Intelligence Agency (CIA)

As the years went on, many of the records were entirely transferred to the CIA under what has been called the "Stargate Collection." This collection encompasses the document cache of records from DIA, CIA, and INSCOM and includes many of the research studies at SRI, funded by the US government. One of the reports found in this collection is a 1995 overall review of the "remote viewing" programs going back through its twenty-year history.

The evaluation was done by the American Institutes for Research, dated September 29, 1995. This document was created to address a request by Congress that the CIA itself continue the "remote viewing" programs. The

American Institutes for Research aimed to evaluate all of the information before them to see if it would be beneficial for the CIA to continue their programs.

You will now see that there were multiple "evaluations" done over the years in regard to "remote viewing." This section has already explored one from 1979 from Systemetrics, but this 1995 document also referred to a mid-1980 review, which concluded, "little or no support was found for the usefulness of many other techniques" when it came to "remote viewing." Here is the entire reference to the mid-1980 review:

> In the mid-1980s, at the request of the Army Research Institute, the National Research Council of the National Academy of Sciences established a blue-ribbon panel charged with evaluating the evidence bearing on the effectiveness of a wide variety of techniques for enhancing human performance. This review was conducted under the overall direction of David A. Goslin, then Executive Director of the Commission on Behavioral and Social Sciences and Education (CBASSE), and now President of the American Institutes for Research (AIR). The review panel's report, Enhancing Human Performance: Issues, Theories, and Techniques, was published by the National Academy Press in 1988 and summarized by Swets and Bjork (1990). They noted that although the panel found some support for certain alternative performance enhancement techniques—for example, guided imagery—little or no support was found for the usefulness of many other techniques, such as learning during sleep and remote viewing.

Now, in 1995, more conclusions were drawn based on another approximately ten years' worth of research. It begs to ask the question, if past evaluations showed no "usefulness" to the research, why would there be another decade worth of funding? Regardless of the real answer to that question, which cannot adequately be addressed, there was another conclusion drawn by the American Institutes for Research:

> Two expert reviewers, one known to be a sophisticated advocate of the study of paranormal phenomena and one viewed as a fair-minded skeptic, reviewed the laboratory experiments conducted as part of the current program that bear on the existence of the remote viewing phenomenon. They focused primarily on recent, better-controlled laboratory studies, drawing from other sources as needed to ensure a comprehensive evaluation of the research litera-

ture. Although the reviewers disagreed on some points, on many points they reached substantial agreement.

The first important point of agreement concerns the existence of a statistically significant effect, which leads to the following finding:

- A statistically significant effect has been observed in the recent laboratory experiments of remote viewing.

However, the existence of a statistically significant effect did not lead both reviewers to the conclusion that this research program has provided an unequivocal demonstration that remote viewing exists. A statistically significant effect might result either from the existence of the phenomenon, or, alternatively, to methodological artifacts or other alternative explanations for the observed effects.

The report then states the final conclusion:

Our conclusion is that at this juncture it would be premature to assume that we have a convincing demonstration of a paranormal phenomenon. In fact, until a plausible causal mechanism has been identified, and competing explanations carefully investigated, we cannot interpret the set of anomalous observations localized to one laboratory with one set of methods. Given these observations, and the methodological problems noted above, we must conclude that

- Adequate experimental and theoretical evidence for the existence of remote viewing as a parapsychological phenomenon has not been provided by the research component of current program. A significant change in focus and methods would be necessary to justify additional laboratory research within the current program.

In summary, two clear-cut conclusions emerge from our examination of the operational component of the current program. First, as stated above, evidence for the operational value of remote viewing is not available, even after a decade of attempts. Second, it is unlikely that remote viewing—as currently understood—even if its existence can be unequivocally demonstrated, will prove of any use in intelligence gathering due to the conditions and constraints applying in intelligence operations and the suspected characteristics of the phenomenon. We conclude that:

- Continued support for the operational component of the current program is not justified.

This report was seemingly the nail in the coffin for about twenty years' worth of research. No government agency, that is known, continued work within the "remote viewing" arena. The CIA, DIA, and INSCOM all had canceled their funding and subsequent programs by the publish date of this report, and clearly, Congress did not get a supporting view that they should fund further research.

The "Stargate Collection," as it became known within the CIA's archive, was ultimately released to the public. Some records took longer than others, but, according to the CIA, the entire collection has entered the public domain; however, some minor redactions remain.

In the private sector, many of the names involved in the Stargate program are still around. There have been no significant changes to the world of "remote viewing" research, but many claim they can teach you the techniques, so you too can be a "remote viewer." Some programs are free, others cost hundreds of dollars.

INDEX

Page numbers for figures are italicized.

ABOUT THE AUTHOR

Starting at the age of fifteen, **John Greenewald, Jr.** was struck with a curiosity that led off a lifelong journey. First researching the UFO phenomenon, Greenewald began utilizing the Freedom of Information Act (FOIA) to hammer the US government for answers, and he targeted every government agency to get them.

As he waited for answers on this niche of the paranormal, he then branched off to investigate nearly every government secret imaginable. He was a sophomore in high school when he first started his trek in 1996, and he archived all of his research on a website that became known around the world as The Black Vault. Today, he has amassed well more than two million pages of declassified records.

His efforts throughout decades of research have been responsible for getting hundreds of thousands of pages into the public domain that might never have seen the light of day. He has appeared on numerous television and radio programs throughout the world and is frequently sourced in various news articles and stories for his archive and his discoveries.